LIVING TOGETHER

Marvin Mitchelson

SIMON AND SCHUSTER · NEW YORK

COPYRIGHT © 1980 BY MARVIN MITCHELSON
ALL RIGHTS RESERVED
INCLUDING THE RIGHT OF REPRODUCTION
IN WHOLE OR IN PART IN ANY FORM
PUBLISHED BY SIMON AND SCHUSTER
A DIVISION OF GULF & WESTERN CORPORATION
SIMON & SCHUSTER BUILDING
ROCKEFELLER CENTER
1230 AVENUE OF THE AMERICAS
NEW YORK, NEW YORK 10020
SIMON AND SCHUSTER AND COLOPHON ARE TRADEMARKS OF
SIMON & SCHUSTER

DESIGNED BY EVE METZ

MANUFACTURED IN THE UNITED STATES OF AMERICA
1 3 5 7 9 10 8 6 4 2
LIBRARY OF CONGRESS CATALOGING IN PUBLICATION DATA

MITCHELSON, MARVIN H
LIVING TOGETHER.

INCLUDES BIBLIOGRAPHICAL REFERENCES AND INDEX.
1. UNMARRIED COUPLES—LEGAL STATUS, LAWS, ETC.—
UNITED STATES.   I. TITLE.
KF538.M57 ·   346.7301'6   80-19768

ISBN 0-671-24981-9

TO SY PRESTEN: whose invaluable momentum and deadlines were indispensable, sincere thanks and appreciation.

TO D. F.: for reasons he knows best.

TO BILL GLUCKSMAN AND ED DE BONIS: loyal associates both.

To the many wives and mistresses I have known—especially to Michelle Triola Marvin, the Joan of Arc of live-in women. Also to Lee Marvin, who helped put a new word in the dictionary—palimony.

CONTENTS

PREFACE

AT A RECENT DINNER PARTY, a man I knew slightly strolled up to me and hissed, "You traitor! Why couldn't you leave well enough alone!" There was a halfhearted smile on his face, but the glint in his eye suggested that he was at least partly serious, that I was somehow, at least to some degree, responsible for the legal problems that have arisen among the legion of unmarried couples who are living together today. I confess to being flattered at such a suggestion, but no person could possibly accept credit for a new social wave of such dimensions, any more than Adam, the first of the unmarrieds, could be blamed for starting the whole thing in the Garden of Eden.

Powerful new forces have weakened the traditional institution of marriage, swept away the taboos against unmarried cohabitation, and the same gale that batters the foundations of matrimony now blows through legal corridors. What affects people affects the law and lawyers. We are of necessity weathervanes turning always to the newest, freshest and most dominant wind of change.

Still, it was the landmark case of *Marvin* v. *Marvin* that first tracked this new wind in a courtroom, and because it "made law" in this new area, I will undoubtedly be damned or praised because of it.

It was this undeniable force that provoked my casual acquaintance's exclamation of "traitor." While he hissed at me, however, his live-in partner gave me a warmer, possibly even grateful, smile. If I am to be blamed by Adam, I suppose I am entitled to the blessings of Eve.

That same gentleman, later in the evening, returned to ask me, surreptitiously, "Listen, what does this new law mean anyway? I am living with a woman." To have explained what the law meant would have taken the entire evening, possibly all night. Here, if he is still interested, is what it is all about.

Greater than the tread of mighty armies is an idea whose time has come.

—*Victor Hugo*

1

"WHY DON'T

I MOVE IN?"

NOBODY REALLY KNOWS how many unmarried couples are living together, but there's no doubt that it's in the millions. Whether it is closer to two million or ten million is an open question. Judging from ordinary conversation, it would seem that couples who have decided to "shack up" far outnumber any other group—especially among young people. Everyone knows couples in his or her own circle who are paired up unofficially. In fact, among young people, the live-ins seem to outnumber the young marrieds by far. Among celebrities, it seems to be well-nigh universal, with the possible exception of Donny and Marie Osmond and the Moonies.

One of the problems of trying to determine the number of unofficial couples is the lack of official records. Marriages are recorded and so are divorces, but Tom does not take out a license when he suggests to Jane, "Why don't I move in?" The Bureau of the Census of the U.S. Department of Commerce does try to count what it calls "unmarried couples"—"households which contain two unrelated adults of opposite sexes."

In 1970, the census takers were able to count 523,000 households of unmarried couples. The bureau's 1978 *Current Population Reports* enumerated 1,137,000 unmarried couples, or an increase of 117 percent. Counting only the 865,000 households consisting of unmarried couples with no children, the increase was 165 percent, which made it the fastest-growing type of household in the nation.

This "official" census figure of 1,137,000 couples—or 2,274,000 persons—is only an approximation, however, as a Census Bureau official conceded. "Not all unmarried couples answer our questionnaires," an official told me. Cohabiting couples also are an extremely impermanent group, with the average lifetime of an arrangement being only about three years, according to one unofficial study in Colorado. After about three years together, a couple often either break up or make it legal and get married.

Census figures also show that the average age for couples who get married is older than it used to be, which suggests that more young couples are living together than ever before. In 1970, the average age for a first marriage among men was 23.2 years, and for women 20.8 years. By 1978, the average for men was 24.2, and for women 21.8. Many of those young people who used to marry young now live together rather than enter into early marriages.

For the record, there were 2,243,000 marriages in 1978, and the Census Bureau found 1,137,000 couples who would officially admit they were living together. There were also 1,128,000 divorces. It is a common generalization that anything can be done with figures, so there's no need to try to build a case that living together will eventually challenge the popularity of marriage. But surely it is clear that the live-togethers comprise a large and growing group.

Who are these 1,137,000 unmarried couples? Only hippies in communes or rock stars or occasional sex-mad drifters? Obviously not. They seem to be from every stratum of society and every age group. A little more than three-fourths of them—865,000—are couples who have no children living with them.

Another 272,000 unmarried couples do have children with them. The statistics also show that in 7 out of 10 unmarried-couple households, both partners are under the age of forty-five, and in the vast majority of cases the two partners were very nearly in the same age range.

So, the first profile of this new unmarried couple emerges: Three-fourths of them are under forty-five and have no children living with them.

Of the 620,000 couples under forty-five who have no children living with them, 236,000 are under twenty-five and 325,000 are from twenty-four to thirty-four. The number in the age range between thirty-five and forty-four suddenly drops to 59,000.

Another image is thus revealed: Most couples live together without children during their early twenties and through their thirties, possibly changing partners from time to time, but as the age of thirty-five comes upon them, live-togethers face a profound challenge. Of the 620,000 couples in the age range under forty-five, only 5 percent fall in the age range of thirty-five to forty-four.

After the critical age of thirty-five among live-togethers, the number remains relatively low during the late thirties, through the forties and into the sixties, where the number begins to climb once more. There were 106,000 couples over the age of sixty-five —more than in the age groups of the late thirties or the forties or the fifties.

This sudden increase in living together among Senior Citizens is the result of Social Security laws, which make it uneconomical —or even economically impossible—for older people to marry because a widow may lose her late husband's pension if she marries again. A widow may choose either her own Social Security pension or one-half of her late husband's pension, whichever is greater. If she picks her husband's benefits and then later decides to remarry, she loses the husband's pension. In other words, if she is collecting $200 a month from her late husband's Social Security pension and she marries a pensioner who is also collecting $200 a month, the two of them will have to get by on only his $200. Naturally, many elderly people forget the marriage license and keep the $400 a month.

In addition to the unmarried couples with no children present, the Census Bureau counted 272,000 couples who had one or more children living with them.

Another yardstick for measuring how many couples are living together is the divorce rate. According to the Census Bureau, the divorce rate is climbing much faster than is the rate of unmarried households. Since 1960, the divorce rate has climbed 157 percent, and from 1970 to 1978 the increase was 91 percent. As of the latest figures, there are 90 divorced persons for every 1,000 persons who are married and living with their spouses.

The rate has risen for both sexes, for blacks and whites and for all age groups. It has risen most dramatically since 1970 and most precipitously among adults aged thirty to forty-four. During the 1960s and 1970s, more couples over the age of forty-five got divorced than under forty-five. But from 1960 to 1978, the divorce rate of couples under thirty climbed by 296 percent. Among those forty-five to sixty-four the increase was 83 percent.

Thus, the figures show that divorce is climbing in all groups, but most rapidly for those under thirty.

"Changes in the frequency with which and ages at which people marry (or dissolve marriages) have a direct bearing on the living arrangements of the population," the Census Bureau's report notes.

With couples waiting longer to marry and divorcing at younger ages than ever before—as well as at all ages more than ever before—there are more and more couples living together without being married. Most of those couples, as we've seen, have no children living with them and are under the age of thirty-five. But there is still a sizable minority who have children living with them and who are older than thirty-five. We see that most of the unmarried spouses are in the same age ranges.

We have, in short, a cross section of American society. The unmarried couple is not a fad limited to kids or involving only fringe people in Haight-Ashbury, Key West, Cape Cod or Greenwich Village. More and more, this is a special group that requires special answers. It has been pretty much beyond the pale of legal and polite society until only recently.

The fact that so many different couples have decided to live

together poses broad questions. In my opinion, this modern phe-
nomenon is caused by a quest for personal freedom without wanting to flee from the pleasures of having a mate. It's an attempt to
refute that once-popular song, ''Love and Marriage,'' which sup-
posedly went together ''like a horse and carriage.'' That idea
apparently went out with that mode of transportation. There is an
emotional and mental assumption that anyone who lives with
another person and isn't bound by a marriage certificate is free to
come and go. Two people begin a relationship without a marriage
license thinking that they can walk away from each other, that
they are not as restricted as they would be if they were legally
married.

''When two people love each other there's no need for a piece
of paper,'' is a theme that runs through many of these live-in
arrangements. The arrangement is conceived as one in which
each gives freely with no strings attached and with guarantees
neither asked nor given. In theory, this rationale envisions two
independent people coming together voluntarily and maintaining
a separate independence during the entire life of the coupling. To
the extent that this idyllic condition exists, it may well be true
that the couple does not need ''a piece of paper.'' Utopia seems
to exist only briefly in human affairs, however. All too soon—in
fact, usually from the very beginning—one of the parties is more
''independent'' or ''equal'' than the other. In a world where true
independence is likely to be economic independence, only two
people who both work or have their own continuing economic
means can remain equally independent. If a woman lives with a
man but does not work herself, she is no longer as independent
as he is. If she has children, her dependence upon him is
deepened even further.

Agreements—or a marriage license—are methods of keeping
the woman independent by guaranteeing her some kind of economic protection. Naturally, such obligations intrude upon the
independence of the man—or the wage-earning spouse. These
are some of the basic elements of the age-old war between the
sexes. A woman with a ''piece of paper'' and/or money of her
own, is more independent and that means she is more equal and
more in control of her own life. An independent woman may

not be as docile, warm, loving and willing to cooperate with a man as a woman who is, as the saying goes, "barefoot and pregnant." Thus it is natural enough for a dependent person—usually the woman—to struggle for some kind of guarantee, while the independent party—usually the man because he is most often the breadwinner—struggles to fend off any guarantees.

Many men avoid marriage because they have the idea that a girl friend will be grateful for small favors, but a wife will feel entitled to them. In Garson Kanin's Broadway comedy, *Born Yesterday,* rough-cut junk dealer Harry Brock shrinks from wedding his live-in girl friend, Billy Dawn, declaring, "I been married. I don't like it. It gets different when you get married. This way, I give her something, I'm a hell of a fella. We get married, she's got it comin', she thinks." The wise old Roman Cato put it this way: "When women come to be our equals, they will be our masters."

Many young people feel that formal marriage has not worked for their predecessors. The divorce rate, as we have seen, is very, very high. It has become an accepted part of the American way of love. Divorce has also become easy to obtain. The last major barriers fell with the widespread passage of "no fault" divorce laws in almost every state, beginning with California, where the Family Law Act became effective on January 1, 1970. Before the "no fault" laws, divorce could be difficult to obtain. In Illinois, one could not divorce a spouse even if that spouse had been committed to a state hospital as hopelessly insane. In New York the only ground for divorce was adultery. (Only Italy, where no divorce was granted for any reason, had more restrictive marriage laws.)

It was divorce laws like the rigid New York code that caused those lurid, sensational divorce trials so dear to the tabloids. When adultery was the only possible ground, there were two alternatives: Either you proved adultery or the two warring spouses lied and said there had been adultery. (Those who could afford it, of course, avoided the problem by going to Reno.) Proving adultery meant hiring private detectives to shadow the suspected wife or husband, and then breaking into the erring spouse's love nest with a photographer to snap compromising pictures. In other states even if there were no requirement to prove adultery, there was still the legal problem of determining who was "at fault,"—the decisive factor affecting the amount of alimony and the division of property.

The easy grounds and the no-fault system of divorce mean that anyone can go to court and get a divorce with very little effort. Not only is it easy, but there's almost no stigma attached. Young people today cannot imagine the lurid aura that once surrounded a woman who was a "divorcée."

That stigma stemmed from a religion-dominated small-town America where everyone knew one another and divorce was almost unheard-of.

In modern America, where most people live in cities, neighbors often do not know one another, even if they live in the same co-op; and there are so many divorces that no one seems to think twice if a couple splits up. So in today's society there's nothing unusual about the breakup of a marriage—no stigma, no penalty and very little interest except on the part of the parties involved. In that sense, we live in a liberated society.

These freedoms—this lack of structure—cause some people to think that the system—marriage—doesn't work anymore.

For the youngest group—the under-twenty-five category—living together means not wanting to be committed, not wanting to be beholden to another person in the way that their mothers and fathers were. They do not want infringements upon their independence, and they want freedom to be individuals. They shudder at phrases such as "til death do us part." They feel it attacks their individuality and reduces their own identities.

"The whole concept of marriage and a family scares the hell out of me at this point in my life," a twenty-one-year-old college student told me. "I wouldn't even want to have a dog. Everything I own fits in the back seat of my Pinto."

Instead of marriage, he lives with a female student and has for three years. "Sometimes, I would like a notarized paper that says he is my official boy friend," she said, striking a note not unusual among many young women.

Another twenty-year-old college student, who has been living with her boy friend for a year, explained, "I believe in marriage, but I'm not ready for it yet. I want a career first."

A couple who had just graduated from the same college and were living together insisted it was mostly a matter of economics. "We share the cost of food and rent," the man said. "It's much cheaper." They both expect to get married eventually, but not necessarily to each other.

This youngest group, the single people under twenty-five, who move in together and then split up again after a year or so without having children, really should face no great problems from a legal standpoint. Usually, not much in the way of property has been accumulated and, therefore, there is little to divide up. They both work, usually, and it can and should be a fairly Utopian existence while it lasts.

The pain of parting for the young singles is usually not economic but emotional. Just because a young couple live together without marriage doesn't mean they'll be spared the pangs of divorce. Parting can be and often is just as anguished for unmarried couples as it is for married couples. A University of Colorado researcher found that the end of a live-in relationship can be very much like going through a divorce. Husband-and-wife kinds of attachments form, dependencies develop and most of the time only one of the parties wants out. But, from a legal point of view, most partings of young singles should be simple.

A couple—both twenty-seven years old—who had lived together for seven years put a down payment on a house in Georgia. The man says he doesn't want to get married because it "would destroy the feeling" of freshness he enjoys. The girl's Irish Catholic family keep pressing for marriage, and the man comments that if his live-in girl friend can't hold out he might marry her. "It'll make me retch, but I'll do it," he says. Once that couple own a house, the institution of property will have entered the picture, and their lives could eventually get more complicated.

In the next age group, those from about twenty-five to thirty-five, the problems of breaking up are usually much greater, because by that time more property and money have been accumulated, and there may be children involved in the arrangement. One or both of the unmarried partners may have been married before and may be paying or receiving alimony or child support.

A couple in San Francisco, Ron and Cindy, own a house together and live there with his thirteen-year-old son and their two dogs. Ron is thirty-nine and Cindy thirty-one. "We might consider getting married if we decided to have a child," said Cindy. "We used to talk about marriage a lot more than we do now." There's another possibly tangled situation if they ever agree to disagree. Ron and Cindy believe that after ten years together their only real problem is, "We don't know what to call each other." They may be right, as long as they never get around to calling each other names from which expletives must be deleted.

The form of address can indeed be confusing when the traditional Mr. and Mrs. husband and wife are dispensed with. Live-ins refer to each other as "roommate," "housemate," or the most popular, "my friend." Oddly enough, very few refer to their cohabitant as "my lover" or "my mistress," as though those two terms are judgmental and somehow cast them into roles they are unwilling to accept. You often hear something as simple as, "I'd like you to meet Jane," or "This is Jim." A little more formal is, "This is Jane Smith." Sometimes you simply have to pick up the obvious hints that reveal she is living there even though you know he's single.

A fifty-five-year-old Los Angeles writer told me that his grown sons—nineteen and twenty—introduce him and his live-in woman by saying, "This is my father's girl friend," or "This is Lorene." The writer introduces her by saying, "This is my girl friend," and she introduces him with, "This is my boy friend," or "This is Harry."

The puzzlement, as often as not, is more of a social delicacy for a parent who has to introduce a daughter or a son who shows up with his or her "friend." "This is my daughter Cecilia, and her . . . uh . . . friend . . . roommate . . . date."

The stickiest moment apparently is the very first meeting between the parents and their child's "friend," which often coincides with their first knowledge of the live-in relationship. One New York City mother told of arriving at the family vacation home in Vermont to find her nineteen-year-old son installed there with his "friend." She and her husband were stunned. "There was this terrible moment when we didn't know what to do. They were not trying to conceal it. So we just welcomed the girl and hoped that everything would come out all right," said Mom. The son and his "friend" later got married. The couple's other sons later brought girls home for weekends to their New York City home, and the parents let them sleep together. "It was a very hard decision," she said. "But I knew they were living together during the week, so what difference did the weekend make?"

Not all mothers are so understanding, of course. One Westchester County mother absolutely refused to allow co-ed sleeping arrangements in her home. "I'd never let any of my children shack up in my house on a weekend," she said. "I insist upon my standards being respected."

When we get to the live-togethers who are thirty-five and older, paradoxically, the situation is often the reverse. A young person may find himself trying to introduce his mom or dad and the parent's "friend" instead of the other way around. Parents in the forties and fifties age range who have only recently accepted the startling idea of their children moving in with roommates of the opposite sex have now taken the plunge themselves.

Eight years ago, a New Jersey housewife with a son and a daughter in their twenties came up against the new morality when her daughter asked if she could share her bedroom with her boy friend. The mother "flipped" and said absolutely not. Today, in her fifties and widowed, the mother lives with a fifty-two-year-old divorced writer in a suburban house they rented together. The recycled live-in widow had the same trouble trying to explain her new life-style to her own seventy-eight-year-old mother. "She's embarrassed. She tells her friends I keep house for an older man," the woman said. She and her new housemate both signed the lease on their rented house and both of them put their names on the mailbox.

Even in the presumably more conservative suburbs, the forty-ish and fifty-ish live-togethers seem to have little social difficulty. "Nobody asks, nobody knows and nobody cares," said a fifty-one-year-old divorcée who has lived with a fifty-five-year-old divorced man for five years.

Nancy, a schoolteacher who has two grown sons, was a recent divorcée when she met Lenny at a party. Lenny, who had three grown children and a teenage son, had just gotten a divorce. During Nancy's divorce, her ex had stormed out of the house and taken along one of their twin beds. When the romance between her and Lenny reached the moving-in stage, Nancy said, "I went out and sold my wedding ring and bought a double bed with the money." Lenny moved in.

The only real problem for Nancy and Lenny was their grown children and their business associates. When Nancy's twenty-four-year-old son came for a weekend visit, the first touchy moment arrived. Lenny decided the only thing to do was to ask the son for his mother's hand.

Bewildered, the son said, "Ask my older brother."

When the older brother arrived for a visit some weeks later—at the same time that Lenny's thirty-year-old daughter put in an appearance—the "situation" arose again. Lenny's daughter was aware of the new live-in arrangement, but not the older brother.

The moment came when the son asked where Lenny was so he could say good-night.

"He's in my bedroom. In bed," said Nancy.

The son's look of confusion prompted Lenny's daughter to drag him toward the door. "Let's go out and have a serious talk," Lenny's daughter said to the shocked son.

They stood out on the driveway for a while, Nancy recalls, and then came back in. "You have our blessing," the son finally managed.

Nancy told her school principal about her new "friend" and the principal merely smiled. Lenny's business associates didn't bat an eye when he told them.

Herb, a fifty-seven-year-old printing executive who had been married twice and had three grown children and five grandchildren, met Sue, fifty, through his sister. Sue, a hospital worker, had never been married and didn't want to get married. She moved in with Herb in his home in Westchester County, a suburb of New York City, and told Herb's daughter, "By the way, I'm moving in with your father." At the hospital when a new boss asked Sue her marital status she replied, "I'm happily living in sin." At Herb's printing company, everybody knows that "the boss's wife,'' as they call Sue, is not really his wife. "I want it that way," said Herb. "If I hid the fact, I'd feel uncomfortable and so would they.''

Another live-in couple in their fifties had been together for five years in Chicago before they moved to a house in a North Shore suburb. Elaine was divorced, with two sons twenty-eight and eighteen, and Bill was separated. His daughter, fifteen, and son, thirteen, live with his estranged wife. When the unweds moved into their suburban home, the only person who couldn't seem to accept it was the woman from the Welcome Wagon.

"The Welcome Wagon lady said, 'It's Mr. and Mrs. what?' and I said, 'No, It's Ms. and Mr.' She couldn't grasp it. She kept filling out all the cards with Mr. and Mrs. Her world just didn't take in people like us.''

In the thirty-five-and-older group—up until the Social Security problem arises in the early-sixties age group—there is a growing problem of property owned by both the male and the female cohabitants. There is also the problem of more and more arrangements in which only the man works and the woman is completely dependent upon him. When a couple both in their twenties break up and both have jobs, both are economically able to continue. But when a woman of thirty-eight who is out of the job market is left alone, the problem is far more difficult. If she has one or more children, the situation can be disastrous.

In the Senior Citizen years, as has been mentioned, a retired person who is collecting either his own or half of his spouse's pension benefits can lose them by marrying another retiree living on Social Security. The variables in the Social Security picture are many, and should be checked with the Social Security Administration.

You will detect a familiar note running through these live-together problems. Just as the first thorny troubles among primitive peoples developed with the rise of the institution of property, the problems of living together also stem from that same institution of property. The troubles start basically with economics.

Agreements between live-togethers are not marriage licenses, which means there are no automatic benefits that flow from the promise to love, honor and share. In a nonnuptial agreement, as the hawker says, "What you see is what you get." They are business agreements, pure and simple, which is why they are treated as contract cases when a dispute arises. So, whatever you agree to is what you are held to—nothing more and nothing less.

Most agreements between live-togethers are for the purpose of limiting the liabilities on the part of one or both of the partners.

The simplest agreement is between two people who desire a "no strings" living arrangement. Both probably work and are therefore economically independent. They make no promises to each other, and exact none. Neither wants nor expects anything from the other except companionship. It's the kind of agreement young couples with no property and no real future plans should find adequate. The agreement carefully sets down what the couples will *not* share. It thoroughly and categorically removes all liability on the part of each to the other.

Here's an example of such a basic "no strings" agreement. It spells out clearly that Roe is only sharing Doe's living facility and is not acquiring any interest in Doe's property, and that Doe is not acquiring any interest in Roe's property. At the end of the *Joint Living Agreement* are Schedule A, on which John lists the property he wants to protect, and Schedule B, on which Mary lists the property she wishes to keep separate. Cash, negotiable securities or paper and significant property should be listed in dollar amounts or approximations. Ordinary possessions such as personal clothing need not be.

JOINT LIVING AGREEMENT

This Agreement is made and entered into this _____ day of _____, 19___ by and between JOHN DOE (hereinafter referred to as "DOE") and MARY ROE (hereinafter referred to as "ROE") with reference to the following facts:

WHEREAS, DOE and ROE are desirous of living together, they may continue to live together in the future, may cease living together, or may in the future become married, although at the present time the parties are not contemplating marriage; and

WHEREAS, since the parties intend to reside together in the same premises, they are desirous of documenting in writing their rights and financial responsibilities, and to disavow any claims or rights that either may have as a result of their cohabitation; and

WHEREAS, the parties have not entered into any understanding and agreement, whether express or implied regarding their respective property interests and rights, except as otherwise provided for herein, it being the intention and understanding of the parties that during the period of time that they may reside together in the future that it is the intention of the parties that ROE is only sharing DOE's living facility and is not acquiring any interests in said property or any other property of DOE and that DOE is likewise not acquiring any interest in any property of ROE; and

WHEREAS, the parties desire to memorialize their agreement with respect to property of each of them, and to evidence their agreement and understanding that all property owned by either ROE or DOE as of the date of this Agreement, whether acquired prior to or during their period of living together, shall remain and be the property of the party acquiring the said property and neither party shall have any right to claim an interest in property owned by the other or any right to receive any financial remuneration from the other for funds allegedly advanced or paid by said party toward the other party's property;

NOW THEREFORE the parties represent and agree as follows:

1. All representations set forth above are true and are incorporated herein by reference;

2. DOE represents that he is the owner of the real and personal property set forth in Schedule A to this Agreement. DOE further represents that although the property set forth in the attached Schedule A, while intending to give an accurate picture of DOE's separate property, may, inadvertently omit some assets, and accordingly DOE does not represent that said list is the total and complete list of his property.

3. ROE represents that she is the owner of the real and personal property set forth in Schedule B to this Agreement. ROE

further represents that although the property set forth in the attached Schedule B, while intending to give an accurate picture of ROE's separate property, may, inadvertently omit some assets, and accordingly ROE does not represent that said list is the total and complete list of her property.

4. The parties mutually declare, acknowledge and agree their understanding, intention and expectation in residing together is as follows:

A. Both ROE and DOE have agreed to keep their respective earnings, income, assets and properties of any nature, or in any place whatsoever as their respective separate property, to be owned by the said party without any claim, right or interest by the other party;

B. all property at any time owned or acquired by either of the parties before or after they live together and all accumulations therefrom, shall be and remain the property of the party owning or acquiring the same, and neither of the parties shall have any claim whatsoever to the other party's property;

C. the respective expectations of both ROE and DOE in cohabiting are solely to share common living facilities and expenses for so long as both shall jointly desire, and provide for the payment of the joint expenses necessary to maintain such common living facilities, during such period of joint residency;

D. neither party expects or intends any partnership, joint venture, resulting or constructive trust, or common enterprise by either of them, in the other party's property or business activities, nor has there been or will any actions of the parties hereafter be construed as being a pooling of any assets or earnings;

E. Neither party expects or agrees to pay or be paid for any services that either may perform for the other, and, in that connection, any aid, comfort, or service given or rendered has been and will be freely and voluntarily given and performed as a gift to the other without expectations or promises of compensation or reward;

F. the conduct of either party in this Agreement in the past, present or future is not meant nor implied to mean or imply any agreement, promise or understanding which controverts in any manner the provisions of this Agreement, unless there is a specific writing by the party to be charged, setting forth a different agreement and understanding than as set forth herein;

G. the parties disclaim that they have any express agreement or understanding that either DOE or ROE has acquired any rights to the property, assets or earnings of the other, or to the increases, profits, or interest of any assets, profits or earnings owned by the other party;

H. the parties specifically acknowledge and agree that no real or personal property has been acquired by the parties jointly, that neither party has spent or contributed money or property for the benefit of the other's property for which any reimbursement is being sought, nor has either party performed any services for compensation from the other;

I. the parties acknowledge that they have not agreed to hold themselves out as husband and wife, have not agreed to matrimonial or other property rights as though they were married, and, as set forth hereinbefore, they have expressly agreed that neither party is acquiring any rights of any sort against the other by reason of the cohabitation;

J. DOE acknowledges that all property of ROE of any nature or in any place as of the date of this Agreement or any property acquired by ROE as a result of the use, investment, reuse or reinvestment of such property is, and shall remain ROE's property and shall be enjoyed by her independent of any right, claim or encumbrance by DOE whether identified in this agreement or not. Included in such property is income, property or assets acquired by ROE through her services, skills, efforts and work together with any increase in value, profits derived from any presently invested capital, existing assets or good will of any business of ROE whether caused by ROE's services, skills, efforts and work, or not;

K. ROE acknowledges that all property of DOE of any nature or in any place as of the date of this Agreement or any property acquired by DOE as a result of the use, investment, reuse or reinvestment of such property is and shall remain DOE's property and shall be enjoyed by him independent of any right, claim or encumbrance by ROE whether identified in this Agreement or not. Included in such property is income, property or assets acquired by DOE through his services, skills, efforts and work together with any increase in value, profits derived from any presently invested capital, existing assets of good will and any business of DOE whether caused by DOE's services, skills, efforts and work, or not.

5. It is the intention of both DOE and ROE that during the period of their cohabitation, although each may voluntarily contribute toward their common living expenses, there is no obligation to do so. Any monies contributed by either DOE or ROE towards said expenses or towards payment of mortgages on real property, real property taxes, payments towards personal property, furniture or furnishings and the like shall not result in a joint ownership interest or the right to claim any reimbursement for the funds so expended, but said property shall continue to be solely the property of the person acquiring the property or in whose name the property stands. However, in the event that the parties should open a joint or joint tenancy bank account, said money shall be considered joint money until such time as it is expended, in which event the foregoing provision of this paragraph shall control.

6. Neither party assumes, nor does either party agree, nor is this Agreement intended to create any obligation, contract or agreement, express or implied, to support the other during the period during which they may cohabit or for any period thereafter. The parties specifically acknowledge and agree that, notwithstanding the fact that ROE or DOE may voluntarily provide the other with support and maintenance during the period that they reside together, such conduct shall not be construed as an agreement, either expressed or implied, to provide the other with support and maintenance, and, each of the parties hereto specifically waives and relinquishes all rights to alimony, support, and maintenance from the other, except in the event of their marriage.

7. Each of the parties hereto specifically acknowledges and agrees that they do not have any right, claim or interest in or to the property of the other, including but without being limited to, rights as an heir or putative spouse, rights to a family allowance, rights in the event of the other party's death, the right to act as an administrator, executor, administratrix, or executrix of the

estate of the other, nor any rights whatsoever by reason of their cohabitation except as otherwise provided for herein. Notwithstanding the provisions of this Agreement and, in particular this paragraph, either party may transfer, convey, devise or bequeath any property to the other or to third parties to be charged. Neither party to this Agreement intends by this Agreement to limit or restrict in any way the right to receive any such transfer, conveyance, devise or bequest from the other, subject to the express condition that it be in writing and signed by the party to be charged.

8. Although Schedules A and B set forth certain items of property which are the separate property of the respective parties, the parties agree that the failure to include on such Schedules any particular items of property which may hereinafter be discovered or remembered by either party shall not change the character of the property, it being the continual intent of the parties that their respective property be and remain claim free regardless of the lack of specification in this Agreement.

9. This Agreement contains the entire understanding of the parties, and there have been no agreements, promises, representations, warranties or inducements, express or implied, or written, other than is expressed and contained herein. All prior conversations of the parties concerning their respective property rights have been referred to, set forth, merged and incorporated in this Agreement.

10. This Agreement may be modified only by a subsequent agreement in writing, signed by both of the parties. It is expressly understood and agreed that any conduct or statements by either of the parties subsequent to this Agreement shall be of no force and effect and shall not be deemed a waiver of modification of all or any part of this Agreement unless the change is acknowledged in writing by the party to be charged.

11. This Agreement shall bind the parties hereto and their respective heirs, personal representatives, executors and administrators.

12. Each part of this Agreement shall be severable from each and every other part of this Agreement and in the event that any part or parts of this Agreement is held to be void or for any

reason not enforceable, such a determination shall not affect the validity and enforceability of the remaining portions of this Agreement.

13. Each of the parties hereto acknowledges that he or she has been advised to obtain counsel to advise said party individually as to the contents of this Agreement, the effect of this Agreement, and the rights which each of the parties may have acquired or lost, by execution of this Agreement. Each of the parties hereto acknowledges that he or she has read this Agreement, has had its contents fully explained to him or her by the respective legal counsel, is fully aware of the contents hereof and the legal effect of this Agreement, that this Agreement has been made freely and voluntarily, and that he or she has requested his attorney to execute and approve this Agreement.

14. It is the intention of the parties that this Agreement shall be governed and interpreted in accordance with the laws of _____.

15. It is the intent of this Agreement to evidence the fact that DOE and ROE have not entered into any express or implied contract, agreement of partnership or joint venture and that there are no constructive or resulting trusts with respect to ownership of property for the benefit of the other, nor that there is any other tacit understanding other than is set forth in this Agreement. In addition, neither of the parties hereto claims, and in fact expressly disclaims any right to receive compensation, or other rights by reason of the nature of their cohabitation.

IN WITNESS WHEREOF the parties have executed this Agreement in ____(City)____, ____(State)____ the day and year first above written.

_____

JOHN DOE

_____

MARY ROE

The undersigned hereby certifies that he is an attorney at law, duly licensed and admitted to practice in the State of

_____; that he has been retained and compensated by MARY ROE, one of the parties in the foregoing Agreement; that he has advised and consulted with MARY ROE in connection with her property rights and has fully explained to her the legal effect of the foregoing agreement and the effect which it has upon her rights as a matter of law; that MARY ROE, after being duly advised by the undersigned, acknowledged to the undersigned that said Agreement truly and fairly sets forth the understanding and agreement which she has had with JOHN DOE with respect to their cohabitation, that she understands that said Agreement memorialized their understanding, and accordingly, she executed the same freely and voluntarily in the presence of the undersigned.

DATED: _____, 19____

_____

Attorney for MARY ROE

The undersigned hereby certifies that he is an attorney at law, duly licensed and admitted to practice in the State of _____, that he has been retained and compensated by JOHN DOE, one of the parties in the foregoing Agreement; that he has advised and consulted with JOHN DOE in connection with his property rights and has fully explained to him the legal effect of the foregoing Agreement and the effect which it has upon his rights as a matter of law; that JOHN DOE, after being advised by the undersigned, acknowledged to the undersigned that said Agreement truly and fairly sets forth the understanding and agreement which he has had with MARY ROE with respect to their cohabitation, that he understands that said Agreement memorializes their understanding, and accordingly, he executed the same freely and voluntarily in the presence of the undersigned.

DATED: _____, 19____

_____

Attorney for JOHN DOE

SCHEDULE A
JOHN DOE's ASSETS AND LIABILITIES
TO REMAIN AS SEPARATE PROPERTY

Cash—$2,500
Residence at 1275 Harmony Lane, Middletown, America
      Equity $28,000.
Furniture and furnishings in residence
1980 Buick, State License Number DOE-12
Matisse print, "Lady With Dog"
Clothes and personal effects
Metropolitan Life Insurance policy, face value $5,000

SCHEDULE B
MARY ROE'S ASSETS AND LIABILITIES
TO REMAIN AS SEPARATE PROPERTY

Cash—$3,000
1979 Toyota, State License Number ROE-12
Wexford Bone China Setting for 12
Jewelry, clothing and personal effects
Life Insurance Policy, face value $7,500

2

"WHY DON'T

YOU MOVE OUT?"

A LIVING-TOGETHER ARRANGEMENT is something like a mystery novel. You don't really get the answers until the end. Only when the relationship breaks up do you find out whether there are problems and how complicated they are. Too often, that's the first time that either you or your partner realizes that you should have had something in writing. That's what happened in *Marvin* v. *Marvin,* the landmark California case I brought on behalf of Michelle Triola Marvin against actor Lee Marvin. Michelle had attempted on occasion to get something in writing but was unable to. We had to argue that in the absence of a written contract, there was an express oral agreement. A lot of "agreements" are like that—they are only thrashed out when somebody says, "Why don't you move out?" Most agreements, in other words, are breaking-up agreements rather than moving-in agreements. The former are apt to be much stormier than the latter. But, then, breaking up is a lot like a divorce, hard to do, and a divorce also comes only at the end of a relationship. Given the blissful state of couples when they first move in together, the likelihood is that most agreements will continue to be reached only upon breaking up.

The road to *Marvin* v. *Marvin* is a trip down the primrose path of American social history. The topic cannot fail to fascinate, because its subjects are sex and money. Out of our Puritan heritage came a guiding principle in the law that sex is legal only within the bonds of marriage.

The cornerstone of the American way of life has always been conceived of as the nuclear family, united in legal and holy matrimony in a three-sided contract consisting of the husband, the wife and the state. Neither the husband nor the wife could decide unilaterally to break the contract, because the third party—the state—had an interest in it. The reasoning was that because the state might have to support a deserted wife and/or children with public funds, it was in the interest of the state to see that the husband provided for his family after a divorce with alimony and/or child support. The marriage bond was further reinforced by religion and custom, both of which exerted social pressure against divorce or abandonment. Because of the state's legitimate interest, states passed legislation to encourage marriage and discourage divorce as a matter of public policy. Religion, again, seconded this secular pressure by proclaiming marriage a sacrament, and admonishing that "Whom God hath joined together, let no man put asunder."

Of course, those who did put a marriage "asunder" were adulterers, and in most states adultery was a felony. Even fornication, which involved no putting asunder, was a minor crime in many states—although violators were seldom if ever prosecuted.

Naturally, even in the early days of the republic, there were a few daring couples who flouted public policy and lived together without marriage. They were social outcasts and matrimonial outlaws. Nevertheless, even outcasts and outlaws can bear children and find themselves deserted.

Branding an immoral woman with a scarlet letter, as was Hester Prynne in the Nathaniel Hawthorne tale, did not solve the problem, nor did putting adulterers in the public stocks.

What was the state to do with adulterers who flouted the public policy?

An abandoned woman with a child in her arms might go to the courthouse and beat on the door, asking for help. "He promised to marry me and to take care of me and my child," she might weep—a cry heard throughout history.

The court of domestic relations demanded that the woman produce her marriage license, because its jurisdiction was limited to married plaintiffs and defendants. If the woman had no marriage license, she had no legal standing, and must seek help elsewhere.

The woman then beat upon the door of the court of common pleas and wailed, "He promised to support me and my child! Isn't that a legal contract?"

The court in its wisdom consulted the public policy, and the social welfare, and established a lasting legal position.

True to the most ancient traditions, American law rested upon the stance of Pontius Pilate and "washed its hands" of the adulterers. They were social outlaws—outside the law—and that was that.

Buttressed by social custom, religion and public policy, the court found that couples who "live in sin" were "guilty" and thus deserving of no legal remedy. Such couples, the law declared, were to be left in the position in which they had placed themselves. They had made their bed, they must sleep in it.

It was a sexual decision, pure and simple, backing up the public policy that demanded that sex be limited to marriage. Unmarried couples who broke secular and religious laws and flouted public policy by "living in sin" were denied the keys to the courthouse door. They could not enter domestic-relations court because they were not married, and they could not enter the court of common pleas because no promise or agreement could be enforced if it involved a couple who were living in sin.

The rationale for this Pontius Pilate stance was that a woman who was living with a man in an unmarried state was a prostitute. The state refused to recognize such liaisons, and would not enforce any agreement that involved sex for pay. Because a woman living with a man in an unmarried state and having sexual intercourse with him was by definition a prostitute, any agreement or promise on his part to pay her was an illegal agreement and thus nonenforceable.

The only legal alternative for a woman who was "living in sin" was to prove that a common-law marriage existed. This was possible in certain states, where common-law marriage was still recognized.

To prove the existence of a common-law marriage, it was necessary to show that there was an intention to marry, that the couple told others that they were married and that they lived together under the same roof as husband and wife in a family type of situation. By such a legal device, a woman who was "living in sin" could be rehabilitated from the state of being a "prostitute" to a legal spouse and thus be deserving of alimony and child support. The third party to the agreement, the state, thus decided the issue.

Legal recognition of common-law marriage was once widespread, established on a state-by-state basis, but recognition of the common-law marriage was outlawed in many states around the turn of the century. In California, the common law was outlawed in 1895 and in Illinois it was scrubbed in 1905. Except in states where common-law marriage is still recognized, a woman living with a man in an unmarried state has no wifely rights.

There is one exception to this general rule that a woman "living in sin" is a "prostitute," and that is if she didn't know she was living in sin: for example, if a wife discovered upon the death of her husband of twenty years that there was another, earlier wife and that her "husband" had never gotten a divorce. From a legal wife, she could be on the spot transformed into a legal "prostitute." The law in its wisdom created a special category for such unfortunates and characterized them as "putative spouses." A putative spouse, being a person who believed he or she was truly married, was thus shown in through the courthouse door to the domestic-relations court.

Achieving a standing as a putative spouse was not automatic, either. Each surprised nonwife had to go to court and plead for recognition as a wronged woman. In a 1948 California case, *Lazzarevich* v. *Lazzarevich*, a "wife" sued her "husband" for divorce only to discover to her dismay that she was not legally married to him. She dropped the divorce suit and lived with Lazzarevich for another year after that, although she knew by that time that she was not really married to him. When they finally separated, the court held that Mrs. Lazzarevich was entitled to the reasonable value of the services she had rendered—less the value of the support she had received—for the years during which she thought she was married. For that final year, however, when she lived with Lazzarevich knowing that she was not married to him, she received nothing. Such is the difference between a putative spouse, who has wifely rights, and a woman "living in sin," who has none.

In recent years, some states have finally given statutory recognition to the putative spouse. In the 1970 California Family Law Act the putative spouse was finally included, and the same recognition was given in the Illinois Marriage and Dissolution of Marriage Act of 1977.

And so we find that wifely shares in divorce cases and in estate settlements are provided for legal wives, and for wives who can be declared legal either as putative spouses or as common-law wives in thirteen states and the District of Columbia. This leaves only the woman (and sometimes the man) who is "living in sin" outside the law dashing frantically from the domestic-relations court to the civil court or court of common pleas crying for help and gaining no admission. Such women and men are legally deemed to be "meretricious spouses." "Meretricious" is defined as "of or pertaining to the characteristics of a prostitute . . . a harlot."

For the meretricious spouse, there was to be no justice in a court. Nor could a woman have her day in court by claiming that a common-law marriage existed if she lived in California, Illinois, New York or thirty-four other states, for in those states common-law marriage was (and is) not recognized. She must be left in the position in which she had knowingly placed herself. Pontius Pilate had washed his hands.

Reflecting the endless variety of human situations, plaintiffs continued to complain that their cases were different, that here was a wronged woman and not a harlot, or that, the issue of harlotry aside, there was still property to be divided and equity to be determined.

When *Marvin* v. *Marvin* arose in 1970, Michelle Triola was in the situation of being a meretricious spouse in a state that did not recognize common-law marriage. She was in the eyes of the law a prostitute, and no agreement she might have could be enforced. The family-law courts were deaf to her pleas; and she could not claim common-law marriage, because it did not exist in California. She could not claim to be a putative spouse, because she knew she was not married to Marvin. (In fact, when she started living with him in 1964, he was still married to Betty Marvin.) The only possible entry into the courthouse was through the civil court with a claim that a contract existed between Michelle and Lee Marvin to share their property.

To grasp how the law works, it should be understood that all laws result from two sources. There is statutory law, placed upon the books by the various state legislatures; and there is "case law," which results from decisions in individual court cases. At any given moment in the continuing evolution of the law, the applicable legal rule is the state statute or the latest case ruling in the field of law concerned. That may sound like Greek at first, but it's relatively clear and simple, as an example or two will show. Anyway, when enough case law develops in a certain field, the laws are codified into a new statute and the evolution continues. A given ruling handed down by an appellate court is the law unless and until it is overturned by a higher court, and should be followed by all judges in that jurisdiction. Some people seem to think that a judge can decide a case as he chooses. Nothing could be further from the truth. He is restricted by the law and the statutes as they exist on the books at that time, and if he reaches the wrong decision—or a decision that one of the litigants believes is wrong—the decision can be appealed. Only when the case finally reaches a state's supreme court must the appeals process stop. If the case includes federal constitutional issues, it can be appealed to a U.S. circuit court of appeals and even to the U.S. Supreme Court. The U.S. Supreme Court, by the way, makes no laws. It only interprets the law and only in cases concerning federal constitutional issues.

At the time that *Marvin* v. *Marvin* arose in 1970, the governing case law in California was what was known as The Vallera-Keene Doctrine, and the statute in effect was the California Family Law Act, which became effective on January 1, 1970.

The Vallera-Keene Doctrine was naturally enough composed of two cases—*Vallera* v. *Vallera* and *Keene* v. *Keene*—and a look at them will give an idea of where the law stood in 1970. Keep in mind that the cases concerned "meretricious spouses" and therefore these cases were heard by civil courts as contract matters rather than matrimonial ones. This is important because although a legal wife can share equally in her husband's property merely by reason of being the man's wife, a partner in a contract-law dispute is not in the same situation. Viewed from such a perspective, the question becomes whether a business partner is entitled to half the business because he or she is having sex with the other partner.

In *Vallera* v. *Vallera,* decided in 1943, the California Supreme Court, in a four-to-three decision, held as follows: "The controversy is thus reduced to the question of whether a woman living with a man as his wife but with no genuine belief that she is legally married to him acquires by reason of cohabitation alone the rights of a co-tenant in his earnings and accumulations during the period of their relationship. It has already been answered in the negative."

In other words, a woman cannot share in a man's community property "by reason of cohabitation alone"—just because she lives with him. There could be no transfer of marriage rights into the civil court or court of common pleas.

The court concluded that "equitable considerations . . . attending the status of marriage . . . are not present in such a case." Unless there was an express written or oral contract, the woman was entitled to share in the property accumulated only "in the proportion that her funds contributed toward its acquisition."

The other half of the doctrine—*Keene* v. *Keene*—was decided in 1962, and in that case the woman-plaintiff sought to avoid the pitfalls of *Vallera* v. *Vallera*. She argued that because she had worked on the man's ranch and enhanced its value, the court should impress a resulting trust upon money from the sale of the property and see that she got her proper share.

The court, however, ruled that providing "services" gives rise to a resulting trust only when the services aid in the acquisition of the property, not in its subsequent improvement.

Case law, then, in 1970 declared that an unmarried woman living with a man could not achieve a share of their accumulated property simply by living with him. If there was an express agreement, she could share to the extent of the agreement. If she contributed money to the acquisition of property, she could share to that extent. If she contributed only housewifely services to the relationship, she could not share in the accumulated money or property, and it was unreasonable of her to expect it. Thus spake Vallera-Keene.

Statutory law in 1970 was codified in the California Family Law Act that became effective January 1, and it was the nation's first "no-fault" divorce statute. The act legitimized the putative spouse and also provided that community property held jointly by married couples should be divided up equally without regard to the "guilt" or "innocence" of either party.

Prior to the no-fault divorce code, a party in a divorce action might get more than half by proving that the other spouse was having an affair or was a drunk or had deserted her or him. Such battles over equity led to acrimonious, mud-slinging divorce trials and uneven distribution of property. The Family Law Act was to brush all such quibbling aside when it came to the division of property accumulated by the married couple together. Farewell to Fault.

The Family Law Act served to further magnify the manifest unfairness of the Vallera-Keene Doctrine. It declared that "guilt" or "fault" could not be used by one spouse to deny the other an equal share of community property. If a spouse could not be penalized for being "guilty," then it seemed to me under equal protection of the law and due process that a nonmarried partner should not be penalized for the "guilt" of "living in sin." Also Vallera-Keene barred an unmarried spouse from recovery only "in the absence of an express contract." Michelle felt she had an express oral contract with Marvin.

On February 22, 1972, I filed a breach-of-contract suit against Lee Marvin in Los Angeles Superior Court on behalf of Michelle, alleging that an express oral contract to share equally in accumulated property existed between them. I asked the court to impress a constructive trust upon the property and to divide it between Michelle and Lee Marvin. Michelle and Lee had lived together from 1964 to 1970, during which time she and the Academy Award–winning actor had accumulated property valued at approximately $2 million.

I had warned Michelle that no unmarried spouse had ever received half of the community property of a man she had lived with, and that we could expect early setbacks. Only a ruling by the California Supreme Court would get her into the courthouse. The first setback came in December of 1973 when we got before a trial judge for the first time. Michelle had said that she and Lee Marvin entered into an oral agreement in 1964 to share any property that they accumulated while they were together. Marvin's lawyers, however, responded that in 1964 Lee Marvin was still married to Betty Marvin, and that such an agreement with another woman was unenforceable. Betty Marvin's divorce was not final until January 5, 1967. The trial court also noted that Michelle was in the position of being a meretricious spouse and that no agreement between her and Marvin could be enforced anyway. The Family Law Act had taken "sin" out of divorce cases, but not out of living together, it seemed. Actually, the trial court did not spell out its reasons but dismissed Michelle's suit because, in effect, the court said it stated "no cause of action" and granted Marvin's motion for "judgment on the pleadings." Back to square one.

Although it seemed that the Family Law Act had not helped Michelle Triola, another California case in 1973 fared much better. That was the case called *In re Marriage of Cary*. Janet Forbes and Paul Cary had lived together for eight years, told everyone they were married, reared four children, bought a house and other property and filed joint income-tax returns. Janet stayed home and cared for the kids, and all the income came from Paul. Here, then, was a meretricious spouse who contributed only wifely services to the relationship and had no express contract; however, a trial court awarded Janet half of the couple's community property when they split up. The Third District Court of Appeal then confirmed the award.

The Cary case is a very important step on the road to *Marvin* v. *Marvin,* and deserves some examination. The court of appeal reasoned that the Family Law Act had taken the "sin" out of "living in sin," and that there was no longer any difference between a putative spouse and an unmarried spouse when it came to division of property. Once fault or guilt was removed, there was nothing to distinguish the property rights of a putative spouse from an unmarried spouse. Because the putative spouse is entitled to half of the property, the court of appeal concluded that under the Family Law Act a nonmarital cohabitant should also be entitled to half of the property accumulated during an actual family relationship.

The Family Law Act, as interpreted in *Cary,* seemed to have changed the position that the "guilty" party should be left in the situation in which she had placed herself.

In any "putative marriage," one of the spouses knows there is no valid marriage and so that partner is "living in sin" as much as any meretricious spouse is. The Family Law Act, however, held that the putative spouse who knew there was no valid marriage, and who was thus "guilty," still received half of the property in a breakup. Why should that "guilty" party be rewarded and a "guilty" spouse in an unmarried cohabitation be punished? The *Cary* court decided that the legislature's intent in passing the Family Law Act was to do away with such distinctions of guilt, reward and punishment.

The court of appeal went on to say: "We should be obliged to presume a legislative intent that a person, who by deceit leads another to believe a valid marriage exists between them, shall be legally guaranteed half of the property they acquire even though most, or all, may have resulted from the earnings of the blameless partner. At the same time, we must infer an inconsistent legislative intent that two persons who candidly with each other enter upon an unmarried family relationship shall be denied any judicial aid whatever in the assertion of otherwise valid property rights."

Cary had definitely tilted the legal alignment, at least at the court-of-appeal level.

Another 1975 case, *Estate of Atherley,* reached the same conclusion based upon the Family Law Act when it decided that a meretricious spouse had the same interests as a putative spouse in the estate of a deceased partner. The *Atherley* ruling also declared, in effect, that it was sex discrimination not to consider "meretricious spousal services such as cooking and housekeeping valuable contributions to the acquisition of assets." It noted that the "typical sex-based division of labor" kept a woman in the home and concluded that a meretricious husband should not be favored over a meretricious wife "simply because in our present stage of social development the husband is usually the single breadwinner."

Thus, two new cases, *Cary* and *Atherley,* both concluded that, under the Family Law Act, property accumulated by nonmarital partners in an actual family relationship should be divided equally.

Using *Cary* and *Atherley* to buttress our case, we filed an amended complaint arguing that even if Michelle and Lee Marvin's express oral agreement of 1964 was nullified by the fact of Marvin's marriage, there was still an agreement in effect for the period after Marvin's divorce in 1967. We sought to share property accumulated during the nearly four years from 1967 until the split in 1970.

But the trial court which had nonsuited us earlier refused to allow an amended complaint. Next stop was the Second District Court of Appeal in Los Angeles, which affirmed the trial court's decision and once more slammed the courthouse door shut. The court of appeal held that Michelle was a meretricious spouse to begin with and so even if she had an agreement it could not be enforced. The court of appeal also rejected the Cary case, saying in effect that it had failed to properly consider the legislative intent behind the passage of the 1970 Family Law Act, and that further it agreed with Marvin's contention that to apply the Family Law Act prior to 1970, the date of its passage, would be to deny Lee Marvin due process of law by applying it retroactively. Once again, we appealed, this time to California's highest tribunal. Constitutional lawyer David Brown joined me on the appeal.

Marvin v. *Marvin* was finally before the California Supreme Court, which I had believed was our destination all along. We presented the state's highest court with three questions:

1. Whether the Vallera-Keene Doctrine should no longer be followed because it furthers no valid state interest, is based upon a double standard of morality which results in discrimination against women, is contrary to present state policy favoring equality between the sexes and is inconsistent with the underlying policy embodied in the Family Law Act.

2. Whether public policy bars enforcement of an express agreement between an unwed couple in a family relationship to pool earnings and share property accumulated merely because the woman's consideration is the provision of typically spousal household services or whether, on the contrary, recovery is barred only when the agreement is, in effect, one for prostitution.

3. Whether the decision of the court of appeal herein, refusing all relief to petitioner in the enforcement either of contractual rights or rights of status arising out of a marital-type family relationship, raises serious state and federal constitutional questions concerning the equal protection of the laws, due process, rights of privacy, association and contract, all of which require hearing and decision by this court.

We argued that it was time to toss the Vallera-Keene Doctrine into the legal dustbin, that it was time for Pontius Pilate to stop washing his hands and pay attention. "Petitioner respectfully contends that the Vallera-Keene Doctrine does not promote any legitimate state interest, but rather is a reflection of a discredited double standard of morality, the result of which is to discriminate against women," ran our argument.

The *Vallera* v. *Vallera* decision, issued in 1943, was a narrow four-to-three ruling, and our argument pointed out that "The dissenting opinion of Justice Curtis in *Vallera*, joined by Justices Carter and Peters, remains a compelling indictment of the majority opinion."

The dissenting justices had observed that the state has determined as part of its fundamental public policy that a wife has a one-half interest in marital property; that the courts have applied the same rule, by analogy, where the parties enter into an "illicit" relationship but believe in good faith that they are married; that the next step was taken in the cases holding that express agreements to share equally in joint accumulations will be enforced; and that the interest of both parties will be protected where they both contribute to the acquisition of property.

The dissenters therefore contended that: "Unless it can be argued that a woman's services as a cook, housekeeper, and homemaker are valueless, it would seem logical that if when she contributes money to the purchase of property her interest will be protected, then when she contributes her services in the home, her interest in property accumulated will be protected."

A rule that treats as valueless a woman's services as cook, housekeeper and homemaker, when rendered as part of a non-marital family relationship, "gives all the advantages to be gained from such a relationship to the man with no burdens," the dissenting opinion went on. It also pointed out that in dealing with a putative marriage, the courts do not treat as valueless a woman's services in the home but divide the property at the termination of a relationship as though it were community property without considering the proportionate contribution of each party to the purchase of the property.

The three dissenting judges concluded: "Unless the underlying purpose be to punish the woman for participating in the illicit relationship—which idea of punishment obviously has no just place in a controversy between two parties equally guilty—why should not the same rule be applied to the instant case?"

The majority opinion in *Vallera* v. *Vallera* permitting the man to "retain the entire fruits of their joint efforts is contrary to the dictates of simple justice," said the dissenters.

There was also an important dissent in *Keene* v. *Keene* by Justice Peters: "The majority opinion adopts a double standard that is neither moral nor legal. It tells us that a woman who has 'sinned' by knowingly entering into a meretricious relationship is not to be permitted to share in property that she helped accumulate, and that all such property is to go to the man involved, even though he has also 'sinned' at least in equal degree."

It cannot be denied that the Vallera-Keene Doctrine discriminates against women, our petition argued, while purporting to apply equally to both sexes. The usual role of the woman in a "meretricious" family relationship is no different from that of a wife—her contributions usually are in the form of household services, whereas the usual role of the man is as wage earner. Yet the double standard of morality implicit in the Vallera-Keene Doctrine rewards the male wage earner who is permitted to retain all property acquired through his wages, while punishing the woman whose household services enhanced the man's ability to acquire property.

Vallera-Keene was also on shaky ground because the courts realized it was unduly harsh and, where possible, they openly invoked the exception that an express agreement existed between the parties in order to give something to the woman. But this application of contractual principles to a family relationship was strained and fictionalized.

The oral agreements in such cases were enforced on the fictionalized theory that the unmarried cohabitants could be viewed as "a joint business enterprise, somewhat akin to a partnership . . . which any two persons (two women or two men, for example) might undertake."

In other words, from the legal point of view sex had nothing to do with couples who were living together. It was all simply a business partnership. Such conclusions are the kind that drove the beleaguered Mr. Bumble in Charles Dickens's tale *Oliver Twist* to mutter, "The law is a ass—a idiot!" But it was reasonable enough, given the fact that a woman living with a man was still persona non grata in a family-law court and had recourse only to the civil court under the breach-of-contract theory.

After arguing that Vallera-Keene should no longer be followed, we urged that express agreements between unmarried couples should be enforced, even if the woman contributed only typical household services. I insisted that Michelle had such an agreement with Marvin, and that her providing him with household services was not prostitution. The court of appeal had thrown us out by saying, "If the living together in a meretricious relationship is a basis for the contract, it is illegal and will not be enforced."

Finally, we argued that depriving a woman of contractual and property rights because she lived with a man outside the bonds of marriage was sex discrimination, a violation of constitutional guarantees of due process and equal protection of the laws, among other things.

It took about a year for the California Supreme Court to digest and decide *Marvin* v. *Marvin*. When it finally ruled on December 27, 1976, the case was over four years old. This drawn-out legal process points up the disparate time gap between long, drawn-out civil court proceedings and getting expeditiously into a family-law court where immediate provisions can be made for temporary alimony and/or child support, and for counsel fees.

When the supreme court ruled, it decided that Michelle Triola was entitled to a trial on her contention that an express oral contract to share community property existed between her and Lee Marvin. That was the main ground for reversal as far as *Marvin* v. *Marvin* was concerned.

But because it also "made law" in the field, clarifying the confusing case law and the interpretation of the California Family Law Act, it became a landmark decision. Those earlier court decisions "hover over the issue in the somewhat wispy form of the figures of a Chagall painting," the court suggested.

To establish a new Marvin Doctrine, the court reached these conclusions in its six-to-one majority opinion:

1. The provisions of the Family Law Act do not govern the distribution of property acquired during a nonmarital relationship; such a relationship remains subject solely to judicial decisions.

2. The courts should enforce express contracts between nonmarital partners except to the extent that the contract is explicitly founded on the consideration of meretricious sexual services.

3. In the absence of an express contract, the courts should inquire into the conduct of the parties to determine whether that conduct demonstrates an implied contract, agreement of partnership or joint venture, or some other tacit understanding between the parties.

4. The courts may also employ the doctrine of quantum meruit, or equitable remedies such as constructive or resulting trusts, when warranted by the facts of the case.

What does it mean? How has the Marvin decision changed the law? You'll remember that Vallera-Keene was the applicable case law, and the Family Law Act was the latest statutory law. The *Marvin* v. *Marvin* ruling held that, first of all, the Family Law Act does not govern nonmarital relationships. So, the change must be in relation to Vallera-Keene.

Vallera-Keene held that property accumulated by an unmarried couple in a family type of relationship was to be divided up if there was an express agreement to that effect. If there was no express agreement, the meretricious spouse was to share in the accumulated property only to the extent that her funds helped in the acquisition of the property. If she contributed only household services during the relationship and had no express agreement, she would get nothing.

Marvin v. *Marvin* declared that each nonmarital relationship must be considered separately, on its own merits. Each individual case is up to the decision of a judge and/or jury after the evidence has been heard. Courts will enforce express contracts unless they are sex-for-pay arrangements.

The major change came in point three. Under Vallera-Keene, the absence of an express contract left the woman in a defenseless situation. *Marvin* v. *Marvin*, however, declared that if there is no express contract, the judge can determine whether there is an "implied contract," based on the conduct of the partners. The trial judge was given sweeping powers to find that there was a partnership, or joint venture, or some other tacit understanding. The judge was mandated by the supreme court to look into the facts and the actions of the parties and reach a fair decision. The judge was empowered to award a judgment to the woman for the reasonable value of her household services less support she had received; he was given power to divide the property or to impress constructive or resulting trusts, depending on the facts and the equities of each case.

The courthouse door was at last open—wide open, in fact—to permit a live-in partner to seek redress through a variety of legal and equitable remedies suitable to each litigant's position.

In fact, in Footnote 25 the California Supreme Court went so far as to invite the trial court to evolve new equitable remedies that would meet the facts and circumstances of a particular case.

Having finally gained access to the courtroom, we went to trial before Los Angeles Superior Court Judge Arthur K. Marshall early in 1979. Judge Marshall heard the trial without a jury.

Michelle Triola, a dancer-singer, met movie star Lee Marvin in June of 1964 on the set of *Ship of Fools,* in which Michelle was an extra and Marvin was a star. Michelle was a divorcée and Lee was still married to Betty Marvin, although that marriage had all but totally disintegrated at the time. "Sexual intimacy commenced about two weeks after their first date," as the trial court papers note, and after that Lee stayed with Michelle in her apartment and then in her rented house off and on. According to Michelle, Lee told her that no "piece of paper" was needed between them.

In December of 1964, Lee went sport fishing in San Blas, Mexico, and Michelle later joined him there. The actor told her he thought his marriage was washed up, and he asked Michelle to live with him. She testified that he said that after the divorce he would be left with only "the shirt on his back." Then he told her —still according to Michelle—"Michelle, what I have is yours and what you have is mine."

Lee later left his wife for good and rented a beach house on the Pacific Coast Highway in Malibu, which he eventually bought. He and Michelle moved into the house and continued to live there for the next six years, until their breakup in May of 1970. During this time, Lee made the movies *Cat Ballou,* for which he won the Academy Award as best actor, *The Dirty Dozen, Hell in the Pacific, Paint Your Wagon* and *Monte Walsh.* From being an actor with only "the shirt on his back" when they started out, he accumulated property and assets during the relationship ultimately valued at approximately $1.5 million at the time of the trial.

During the time they lived together, said Michelle, Lee induced her to give up her career as a singer and dancer to spend full time taking care of him—as a companion, housekeeper and cook.

In 1966, he told her not to worry about a career. "I don't know what you're worrying about. I'll always take care of you," he told her in the presence of her manager, Mimi Marleaux, who testified at the trial.

Lee and Michelle traveled together—to London during the making of *The Dirty Dozen,* to Micronesia during the making of *Hell in the Pacific,* to Baker, Oregon, during the making of *Paint Your Wagon,* and to Tucson, Arizona, during the making of *Monte Walsh*—and while on those latter three trips they maintained joint bank accounts. Also while on the trips, and also while living at home, they lived together in a confidential relationship, often in the manner of husband and wife. During these trips, Michelle sometimes encountered problems with passport and customs officials and hotel desk clerks. In 1970, I helped her legally change her name from "Triola" to "Marvin."

Our case, in summary, was that an express oral contract was formed when Lee asked Michelle to live with him and said, "What I have is yours, and what you have is mine." He also introduced her publicly—but not always—as Mrs. Marvin. The contract consideration was that she would provide household services and give up her career. He would contribute his earnings. The property to be divided was the $1.5 million that had been accumulated during their almost seven years together, and its ultimate value we claimed by the time the trial actually commenced.

We also argued that, in the absence of an express oral contract, the court should find that an implied contract existed, based upon the fact that Lee's actions showed that he intended to share with Michelle.

After a lengthy trial, during which Lee testified that he had not intended to nor in fact did he have an agreement with Michelle and that although he felt affection for her sometimes, he only really wanted her "in bed," Judge Marshall took up the following knotty legal problems:

1. *Is There An Express Agreement?* Judge Marshall held that "it is not reasonable" for a person to believe such remarks as, "What I have is yours and what you have is mine." There must be mutual consent and an intent to contract, and both parties

must have the same understanding of the agreement. "It is more reasonable to conclude that the declaration is simply hyperbole typical of persons who live and work in the entertainment field," he concluded. Thus, legally, there was no express oral agreement.

2. *Is There An Implied Contract?* Judge Marshall noted that Lee kept his property in his own name, filed a separate tax return, had separate bank accounts (except on trips "for convenience"), and that giving up her career was not adequate consideration because it was not much of a career anyway. As for providing him with homemaking services, he observed: "Those services may be rendered out of love or affection and are indeed so rendered in a myriad of relationships between man and woman which are not contractual in nature." Thus, legally, he found that no implied contract existed either.

It was at this point that the California Supreme Court ruling—the Marvin decision—was applied. "If no contract, express or implied, is to be found, the supreme court adjures the trial court to ascertain whether any equitable remedies are applicable," Judge Marshall declared in his decision. "The court is aware that Footnote 25 urges the trial court to employ whatever equitable remedy may be proper under the circumstances.

"In view of these circumstances, the court in equity awards plaintiff $104,000 for rehabilitation purposes so that she may have the economic means to re-educate herself and to learn new, employable skills or to refurbish those utilized, for example, during her most recent employment and so that she may return from her status as companion of a motion picture star to a separate, independent but perhaps more prosaic existence."

The award was considered to be "approximately equivalent to the highest scale that [Michelle] ever earned as a singer, $1,000 per week, for two years."

The court's award resembled alimony (dubbed "palimony" by the media), the first award of its kind, another unique result of *Marvin* v. *Marvin*.

What might be learned from the Marvin decision and its actual application in a trial? First, it should be understood that although the *Michelle Triola* v. *Lee Marvin* case is over, the Marvin decision remains. Other cases will follow—indeed, have followed—and the results will vary with each individual case according to the evidence.

Also, it should be clear that even with the broad sweep of power given to trial judges by the Marvin decision it is not easy to prove that express or implied contracts exist if there are disputes about them. If one partner keeps his property, his bank account, his income tax returns separate, those facts may weigh more heavily in an actual trial than any remembered spoken words which may be afterward denied. Judge Marshall noted that it is "not reasonable" to believe pillow talk.

There is also a paragraph in Judge Marshall's decision that might serve as an object lesson for people involved in such situations. It concerns Michelle's testimony that during the relationship she asked Lee for a written agreement in case of his death. According to Michelle's testimony, he responded that he said it was not necessary—"You're taken care of"—and she believed him. Neither the meek nor the gullible shall inherit the earth.

A single woman who decides to live with a man who is married but separated from his wife needs more protection than does a single woman who moves in with a single man. The two singles might eventually marry, but the unattached female living with an attached male would be wise not to consider that likelihood.

Here's an example of an agreement between a married man named John and a single woman named Mary. Unlike the two singles who agreed to share nothing but a place of habitation, John agrees to pay Mary $5,000 and to put an additional $500 a month into her bank account if she puts in an equal amount. Because Mary cannot hope to achieve marital status with a man who is married, John agrees to give her a $50,000 life insurance policy. Because John is married, he wishes to limit his liabilities toward Mary. Mary, on the other hand, needs some protection. This agreement, like any live-together contract, is still basically an agreement to avoid liabilities. As Paragraph 4C states: "The respective expectations of both John and Mary during their period of cohabitation are solely to share John's living facilities for so long as both jointly desire."

Mary's chances of obtaining any of John's property if and when they eventually split are virtually nonexistent, because she is entering into a living-together arrangement with a married man and with her eyes wide open. The agreement notes that John's property is held in conjunction with his wife. For these reasons, no lists of property to be kept separate are drawn up, as Paragraph 10 declares.

AGREEMENT

This Agreement is made and entered into this ____ day of _____, 19____, in _____*(City)*_____, _____*(State)*_____, by and between JOHN DOE (hereinafter "JOHN"), and MARY ROE (hereinafter "MARY") with reference to the following facts:

WHEREAS, JOHN and MARY have had a dating relationship for several years and have recently commenced living together and are presently both desirous of living together in the future. The parties are not married nor are they presently contemplating marriage; and

WHEREAS, because JOHN and MARY are presently desirous of and intend residing together at certain premises owned by JOHN and they are desirous of documenting in writing their rights and financial responsibilities, and to disavow any claims or rights that either may have as a result of their cohabitation; and

WHEREAS, the parties have not entered into any express or implied understanding or agreements regarding their respective property interests and rights, except as provided for in this Agreement, it being the intention and understanding of the parties that during the period of time that they may reside together it is the intention and agreement of the parties that MARY is only sharing JOHN's living facilities and is not acquiring any interest in said property or any other property of JOHN, except as otherwise provided for in this Agreement, and that JOHN is likewise not acquiring any interest in any property of MARY; and

WHEREAS, the parties to memorialize their agreement with respect to the property of each of them, and to evidence their agreement and understanding that all property owned by either

JOHN or MARY, whether acquired prior to or during their period of living together shall remain and be the property of the party acquiring the said property and further, neither party shall have any right to claim an interest in any property belonging to each of them or any right to receive any financial remuneration from the other for funds allegedly advanced or paid by said party for the other party's property;

NOW, THEREFORE, THE PARTIES REPRESENT AND AGREE AS FOLLOWS:

1. The representations set forth above are true and are incorporated herein by reference.

2. The parties acknowledge and agree that JOHN is presently married although he is separated from his present wife; and the fact of JOHN's marriage shall have no bearing on the provisions of this Agreement.

3. JOHN warrants and represents that he, either individually or in conjunction with his wife, owns substantial real and personal property, including, but not limited to, an ownership interest in property in _____, _____ and elsewhere, partnership and interests in various partnerships, ownership interests in various corporations and an ownership interest in a real estate corporation involved in the acquisition, development and management of real property. JOHN represents and acknowledges that said assets identified above are not a list of every asset owned by him and, accordingly, he does not represent that the property listed herein is a total and complete list of property owned by him.

4. The parties mutually declare, acknowledge and agree that their understanding, intention and expectation with respect to the respective rights and interests resulting from their residing together is as follows (except as might otherwise be specifically set forth in this Agreement):

(a) Both JOHN and MARY have agreed to keep their respective earnings, income, assets and property of any nature or in any place whatsoever as their respective separate property, to be owned by the said party without any claim, right or interest by the other;

(b) all property at any time owned or acquired by either of the parties before or after they reside together and all accumulations therefrom, including income derived from the operations of said property, shall be and remain the property of the party owning or acquiring the same, and neither of the parties shall have any claim whatsoever to the other party's property;

(c) the respective expectations of both JOHN and MARY during their period of cohabitation are solely to share JOHN's living facilities for so long as both jointly desire. In that connection, MARY acknowledges and agrees that the parties are presently planning to occupy certain real property acquired and owned by JOHN at _____. In that connection, MARY acknowledges and agrees that if, in the future, JOHN should determine that he is not desirous of their continuing to cohabit, that she will vacate his residence (upon having been given at least 90 days written notice) if requested to do so by JOHN;

(d) neither party expects or intends any partnership, joint venture, resulting or constructive trust or enterprise in the other party's property or business activities, nor has there been any intention of nor will there be any pooling of any assets or earnings;

(e) neither party expects or agrees to pay or to be paid for any services that either may perform for the other, and, in that connection, any aid, comfort or service given or rendered has been and will be freely and voluntarily given and performed as a gift to the other, without expectations or promises of compensation or reward;

(f) the conduct of either party to this Agreement in the past (including having lived together for various periods of time), present, or future, is not meant or implied to mean or imply any agreement, promise or understanding which contraverts in any manner the provisions of this Agreement, unless there is a specific writing by the party to be charged setting forth a different agreement and understanding than as set forth herein;

(g) the parties expressly disclaim that they have any express agreement or understanding to the effect that either JOHN or MARY has acquired or will acquire any rights to the property, assets or earnings of the other party, and expressly acknowledge and agree that there is no such agreement;

(h) the parties specifically acknowledge and agree that no real or personal property has been acquired by, or is in the process of being acquired by, the parties jointly; that neither party has spent nor contributed money or property for the benefit of the other's property for which any reimbursement is being sought, nor has either party performed any services for compensation from the other;

(i) the parties acknowledge and agree that they have agreed not to hold themselves out as husband and wife; have agreed that neither party has any matrimonial or other property rights as though they were married; that if in the future they should hold themselves out as husband and wife then such holding out shall not alter, amend, or change their rights as specifically delineated in this Agreement; and, as set forth hereinbefore, the parties have expressly agreed that neither party is acquiring any rights of any sort against the other by reason of their relationship and cohabitation, except as otherwise provided for herein;

(j) MARY acknowledges that all property of JOHN of any nature or at any place as of the date of this Agreement, or any property acquired by JOHN as a result of his income, the use, investment, reuse or reinvestment of his property, is, and shall remain, JOHN's property and shall be enjoyed by him independent of any right, claim, or encumbrance of MARY, whether identified in this Agreement or not. Included in such property is income, property or assets acquired by JOHN through his services, skills, efforts and work, together with any increase in value or profits derived from any presently invested capital, existing assets or good will of any business of JOHN, whether caused by JOHN's services, skills, efforts and work, or not;

(k) JOHN acknowledges that all property of MARY of any nature or at any place as of the date of this Agreement, or any property acquired by MARY as a result of her income, the use, investment, reuse or reinvestment of her property, is, and shall remain, MARY's property and shall be enjoyed by her independent of any right, claim or encumbrance of JOHN, whether identified in this Agreement or not. Included in such property is income, property or assets acquired by MARY through her services, skills, efforts and work, together with any increase in value, profits derived from any presently invested capital, existing assets or good will of any business of MARY, whether caused by MARY's services, skills, efforts and work, or not.

5. It is the intention of both JOHN and MARY that during the period of their residing together, although JOHN may voluntarily contribute toward their common living expenses or MARY's living expenses, there is no continuing obligation on JOHN's behalf to do so. Any monies contributed by either JOHN or MARY toward the said living expenses or toward payment of mortgages on real property, real property taxes, expenses of operating real property, payments toward personal property, furniture and furnishings alike, shall not result in a joint ownership interest or the right to claim any reimbursement for the funds so expended, but said property shall continue to be solely the property of the person acquiring the property or in whose name the property stands. In the event the parties shall open a joint or joint tenancy bank account, however, said money shall be considered joint money until such time as it is expended, in which event the foregoing provisions of this paragraph shall control.

6. Neither party assumes, nor does either party agree, nor is this Agreement intended to create any obligation, contract or agreement, express or implied, to support the other during any period whatsoever.

7. The parties acknowledge and agree that neither of them is obligated to support the other during the period during which they may reside together or for any period thereafter. The parties specifically acknowledge and agree that, notwithstanding the fact that JOHN or MARY may voluntarily provide the other with support and maintenance during the period that they are jointly desirous of residing together, such conduct shall not be construed as an agreement, either express or implied, to provide the other with support and maintenance, and each of the parties hereto specifically waives and relinquishes all rights to alimony, support and maintenance from the other, funds for rehabilitation, and the like, except in the event of their marriage, in which event the provisions of this Agreement shall cease and terminate as of the date of the said marriage, but shall be effective for all periods previous thereto.

8. Each of the parties hereto specifically acknowledges and agrees that they do not have any right, claim or interest in or to the property of the other, including, but without being limited to, rights as an heir or putative spouse, rights to a family allowance, rights in the event of the other party's death, the right to act as an administrator, executor, administratrix or executrix of the estate of the other, nor any rights whatsoever by reason of their relationship and/or cohabitation, except as otherwise provided for in this Agreement. Notwithstanding the provisions of this Agreement, and, in particular this paragraph, either party may transfer, convey, devise or bequeath any property to the other. Neither party to this Agreement intends by this Agreement to limit or restrict in any way the right to receive any such transfer, conveyance, devise or bequest from the other, subject to the express condition that the transfer, conveyance, devise or bequest from the other be in writing and signed by the party to be charged.

9. Notwithstanding the previous provisions of this Agreement, JOHN has agreed to the following provisions for the benefit of MARY:

(a) In the event the parties are jointly desirous of continuing to reside together thirty (30) days after the date of this Agreement, JOHN shall transfer to MARY the sum of $5,000 to be put in a savings account for her future benefit;

(b) For so long as both parties are jointly desirous of continuing to reside together, JOHN may, at his discretion, pay for and maintain in full force and effect, with MARY as beneficiary and owner (so long as JOHN is insurable), a policy or policies of term life on his life, with a total face value of $50,000, unless increased from time to time by JOHN;

(c) For so long as both parties are jointly desirous of residing together, or until otherwise decided by JOHN, whichever should occur first, and as an inducement to MARY to continue to work, earn funds, and increase her separate estate, JOHN shall, during each month that the parties reside together, deposit up to $500 into a savings account designated by MARY, provided that MARY matches the deposit with an equal amount of funds obtained by her from her employment.

All sums referred to in this paragraph are intended to and shall remain MARY's separate property, in furtherance of the provisions of this entire Agreement.

10. Although the parties have not specifically delineated the property which is their respective separate property, the parties acknowledge and agree that that fact shall not change the character of the property, it being the continual intent of the parties that their respective property and income shall be and remain claim free, regardless of the lack of specification in this Agreement.

11. This Agreement contains the entire understanding of the parties, and there have been no agreements, promises, representations, warranties, inducements, expressed or implied, written or oral, other than as set forth, expressed and contained herein. All prior conversations of the parties concerning their respective property rights have been referred to, set forth, merged and incorporated in this Agreement.

12. This Agreement may be modified only by a subsequent agreement in writing, signed by the party to be charged. It is expressly understood and agreed that any conduct or statements by either of the parties subsequent to this agreement shall be of no force and effect, and shall not be deemed a waiver or modification of all or any part of this Agreement, unless the change is acknowledged in writing by the party to be charged.

13. This Agreement shall bind the parties hereto and their respective heirs, personal representatives, executors and administrators.

14. Each part of this Agreement shall be severable from each and every other part of this Agreement, and, in the event that any part or parts of this Agreement shall be held to be void or for any reason unenforceable, such determination shall not affect the validity and enforceability of the remaining portions of this Agreement.

15. It is the intention of the parties that this Agreement shall be governed and interpreted in accordance with the laws of the State of _____, wheresoever the parties may reside during the period that they are jointly desirous of residing together.

16. It is the intent of this Agreement to evidence the fact that

JOHN and MARY have not entered into any express or implied contract, agreement, partnership, or joint venture, and that there are no resulting or constructive trusts with respect to the owner-ship of property for the benefit of the other, nor that there is any understanding other than as set forth in this Agreement. In addi-tion, neither of the parties hereto claims, and in fact each of the parties expressly disclaims, any right to receive compensation or other rights by reason of their relationship.

17. Each of the parties hereby acknowledges that he or she has been advised to obtain counsel to advise said party individually as to the contents of this Agreement, the effects of this Agree-ment, and the rights which each of the parties may have acquired or lost by the execution of this Agreement. Each of the parties hereto acknowledges that he or she has read this Agreement, has had its contents fully explained to him or her by his or her respec-tive legal counsel, is fully aware of the contents hereof, and the legal effect of this Agreement, that this Agreement has been made freely and voluntarily, and that he or she has requested his or her respective attorneys to execute and approve this Agreement.

IN WITNESS WHEREOF, the parties have executed this Agreement in _____(City)_____, _____(State)_____, the day and year first above written.

_____

JOHN DOE

_____

MARY ROE

The undersigned hereby certifies that he is an attorney-at-law, duly licensed and admitted to practice in the State of _____; that he has been retained and compensated by JOHN DOE, one of the parties to the foregoing Agreement; that he has advised and consulted with JOHN DOE in connection with his property rights and has fully explained to him the legal effect of the foregoing Agreement and the effect which it has upon his rights as a matter of law; that JOHN DOE, after being duly advised by the undersigned, acknowledged to the under-signed that the said Agreement truly sets forth the understanding and agreement which he has had with MARY ROE with respect to their cohabitation; that he is agreeable to the provisions of said Agreement; that he understands the terms of said Agreement; that said Agreement memorializes his understanding with MARY; and that accordingly he executed the same freely and voluntarily in the presence of the undersigned.

Dated: _____

By _____
     ATTORNEY FOR JOHN DOE

The undersigned hereby certifies that he is an attorney-at-law, duly licensed and admitted to practice in the State of _____; that he has been retained and compensated by MARY ROE, one of the parties to the foregoing Agreement; that he has advised and consulted with MARY ROE in connection with her property rights and has fully explained to her the legal effect of the foregoing Agreement and the effect which it has upon her rights as a matter of law; that MARY ROE, after being duly advised by the undersigned, acknowledged to the under-signed that the said Agreement truly sets forth the understanding and agreement which she has had with JOHN DOE with respect to their cohabitation; that she is agreeable to the provisions of said Agreement; that she understands the terms of said agree-ment; that said Agreement memorializes her understanding with JOHN; and that accordingly she executed the same freely and voluntarily in the presence of the undersigned.

Dated: _____

By _____
     ATTORNEY FOR MARY ROE

3

LIVING TOGETHER

BEFORE MARRIAGE

A LOT OF MARRIAGES break up because the woman feels she is not being treated as a wife, or the man feels he is not being treated as a husband. A lot of live-ins break up because a woman feels she *is* being treated like a wife, or the man finds out he is just as henpecked as any trapped husband.

"If I wanted to iron his shirts and cook his meals, I would have gotten married," a disillusioned live-in woman complains.

"If I wanted to be told when to get home every night, I would have taken on a wife," the indignant man sneers.

The simple truth is that living together is often and virtually the same as being married, and the longer a couple stays together the more like marriage it truly is. Living together "completely free" is, I think, something that proves to be only a concept after a while. Living together binds a couple to each other. Their feelings, their relationship, their dependence, their love, tie the invisible knot. The ceremonies that some unmarried couples go through are, indeed, as formal as many marriages used to be. In reality, a "consensus" to live together is a marriage in the true sense of the word if not in the legal sense. Couples who say they do not need "a piece of paper" to be committed speak more truly than they might realize. They could as easily say they are married even without that piece of paper. In fact, Webster's Dictionary gives as one of the definitions of marriage "an intimate or close union." Nowhere within that definition is there a prerequisite for formalized licensing by the state.

Any discussion of living together and/or marriage is an exercise in emotional relativity, where reality, like beauty, becomes something in the eye of the beholder. Opposites abound. One person's reality is another's illusion. We all know that love is blind, which possibly is another way of saying that those in love are quite capable of endless self-delusion. Couples who decide to move in together are usually in love just as marrieds are and, therefore, at least partially emotionally deranged. They do not consider that they are entering into a contract, which is something built into a marriage. The very thought of sullying their love with a crass document seldom, if ever, enters their ecstatic minds. If it does, they are likely to dismiss the idea with indignation. Implicit in the very concept of living together, in fact, is sometimes a desire to escape such ties and stipulations. Should a couple who is shunning a marriage contract enter into a nonmarriage contract? The likelihood that they are entering into a contract—or an agreement—of some kind whether they sign "a piece of paper" or not usually does not occur to them. Not, at least, until the end of the affair.

What constitutes a valid agreement between a man and a woman that will be enforced in the event that they separate or divorce or one dies? If you are legally married, you, of course, have an agreement. If you are not married, you have to determine whether there is an agreement or not. You either have one or you do not.

Remember that even if you are married, you do not automatically share fifty-fifty in everything your spouse owns. In community-property states, you share equally in everything you and your spouse have accumulated during your years together. If a man dies without having made a will and without an agreement with his wife, she may be entitled to at least one-half of his estate in community-property states, or a third of his estate as a "widow's share" in other jurisdictions.

But, a spouse does not automatically become half owner of everything the other partner owns. If Sally marries Bill and he owns an ancestral mansion handed down from his father and grandfather, that mansion remains his sole property even after he marries unless he decides to put his new wife's name on the title deed or convey an interest to her in some other recognized legal manner. In the same way, if Sally owns half of a textile mill in her own name, she does not automatically yield up half ownership by marrying Bill. In other words, what each partner owns separately at the time of the marriage remains his or her separate property unless they choose to change that situation. And if, after they are married, Bill inherits a Picasso from his grandfather, that, too, remains his personal property and not something owned by him and Sally. People who are married can continue to own separate property and to acquire additional separate property.

If, however, Bill starts a grocery store after he marries Sally and it grows into a supermarket chain during his thirty years of marriage to Sally, she will be entitled to half of that property if he dies or they divorce. Just because you are married does not mean that you cannot own property separately, nor does it mean that what's yours is hers and vice versa. Couples about to be married sometimes execute agreements, too, particularly if either party happens to own property.

Such agreements, known legally as "ante-nuptial" or "prenuptial" agreements, are designed to keep property separate despite a legal marriage. In earlier, more class-conscious eras, persons of rank and property who married persons of lower station entered into what were known as "morganatic marriages." Under a "morganatic marriage," the person of lower station agreed that neither she nor her children would have any right to the eminent person's rank or property.

So a married person has an agreement by virtue of being married.

A legally recognized putative spouse who believes in good faith that he or she is married has an agreement too.

A common-law-marriage spouse has an agreement if he or she lives in one of the fourteen jurisdictions that recognize common-law marriage. Those jurisdictions are Alabama, Colorado, the District of Columbia, Georgia, Idaho, Iowa, Kansas, Montana, Ohio, Oklahoma, Pennsylvania, Rhode Island, South Carolina and Texas.

Legal recognition of a putative or common-law marriage is not automatic, but must be established by the evidence. It is not just the number of years a couple has been together that proves the existence of a common-law marriage—although the longer they are together, the more intent is shown—but the actions of the parties.

If a state recognizes common-law marriage, then the two partners must show their intention to be treated as married. They must have lived together under the same roof, and it helps to have told relatives and the public that they are man and wife. A couple thus united in a common-law-marriage state may be as married as any couple who went through a ceremony and have a marriage contract between them. If they afterward move to, say, New York or California or any state that does not recognize common-law marriage, they are nevertheless still treated as though they are legally married. And if a couple united in common-law marriage wish to split up and remarry, they must get a divorce even though they may now reside in a non-common-law state. A couple cannot be united by common-law marriage, by the way, if either is already married and that marriage has not been legally dissolved. And they cannot be united in common-law marriage if they live from the outset in a state that does not recognize it, no matter how much one or both of them may wish to be.

In a 1949 Wisconsin case, *Smith* v. *Smith,* a woman lived with a man for ten years after being assured by the man that they had a valid common-law marriage. Then the woman discovered that common-law marriage is not recognized in Wisconsin, and she demanded that he marry her. He promptly deserted her. The woman, who had put a good bit of her earnings into the "family" business—which was in his name, as was some real estate—then brought suit for a division of the "marital property." But in Wisconsin in 1949 a woman living in sin was legally a meretricious spouse.

The Wisconsin Supreme Court declared: "In such a case, it is a well-settled rule that a court of equity leaves the parties to such a situation just where they placed themselves and as the court found them. Its doors are closed to any applicant for relief from or under such a contract.''

Although agreements to share accumulated property have always existed between married couples, putative spouses and common-law-marriage partners (where recognized), the question of sharing between unmarried partners was for many years stained by the blot of illicit sex. If sex was deemed to be the key element of an agreement, it was unenforceable.

Gradually, an evolution in the law took place. In some jurisdictions and in certain types of cases it was conceded that two people could possibly have sex together and still maintain a separate business relationship.

If a man was having sex with a woman and at a later time she moved in with him and began caring for him, the law sometimes and inconsistently concluded that the woman was performing this work gratuitously, out of love and affection for him. Therefore, any agreement between them was so involved with sex that it was deemed meretricious and she could not share in his property as a result.

But, if a man hired a woman to clean and cook for him, and afterward seduced her into having sex with him, some courts bent on seeking an equitable result considered that a housework contract could still exist between them. The sex was incidental in that arrangement. Eventually, the concept of a divisible contract evolved. There was a sexual contract that was meretricious and unenforceable, and there was also a separate property agreement that was enforceable.

Legal precedents have now been established in many states that agreements between unmarried couples will be enforced, and that a fair division of accumulated property may be made. It has been held that a woman who stays at home and does not contribute money or property to the partnership will nevertheless share in the couple's property.

But, agreements between nonmarital partners are not "automatic" in any sense of the word. They must be proven by evidence. An agreement may exist whether it has been specifically stated or written down or only "understood."

I have always called ante-nuptial types of agreements between nonmarried persons "nonnuptial agreements." The question is whether the agreement is legal, whether it is binding and valid, whether it will hold up in court. If the agreement is legally binding and valid, you are held to the terms of that agreement.

There are two types of agreements:

1. An express agreement (or contract)
2. An implied agreement (or contract)

An "express" agreement simply means that an agreement has been discussed and its terms defined and openly arrived at between the parties. It can be either an "oral" agreement or a written agreement. As long as it is an arm's-length agreement— meaning that neither party is being unduly influenced or coerced by the other—it can be an express agreement.

An implied agreement, of course, is the other side of the same coin; it is one that has never been put into words or written down but one that may be clearly inferred by the actions of the two parties. For example, two people hold a bank account jointly and treat such an account in every respect as though they share equal control and use of it.

Naturally, if you have everything in writing, you have the best possible protection. But the fact that an agreement is in writing does not in itself make it binding. It must also be a fair agreement.

It has now been established that there can be what is called a "confidential relationship" between two people who are living together but are not married. Prior to *Marvin* v. *Marvin*, in the eyes of the law, there could be a confidential relationship only between two people who were married. A confidential relationship means that two people are so close to each other that they are under each other's influence, control or domination. When people love each other they are influenced by each other. They trust each other. They do things by virtue of the trust and confidence they place in the other party. The Marvin case established in clear, unmistakable language that you don't have to be married to have a confidential relationship. Many couples who live together are just as confidentially involved as couples with a marriage license in a drawer or on the wall. The question here is simply whether one party took advantage of the other due to their confidential relationship to get him or her to enter into a written agreement that is not a fair one. If something like that happens, a written contract can be set aside by the court or tryer of fact because of a lack of understanding on the part of one of the parties, or because of fraud, mistake, ambiguity in its essential terms or undue influence.

To use an extreme example, let us say a sophisticated world traveler, a lawyer who has successfully practiced divorce law for twenty years, meets a seventeen-year-old girl from an isolated hollow in the mountains. He persuades her to live with him.

Now, our knowledgeable man of the world sits down with the young mountain flower and says, "Let's have this agreement," and he draws up a list of all the things he wants her to do. She is to cook and clean and attend to all his desires and needs. (Remember, sex doesn't count here.) The agreement concludes by putting down his side of the bargain. "For this, I will give you $1 a month, plus my body." If the young innocent signs this agreement and lives with the lawyer until she is thirty-five, faithfully performing all these wonderful duties, a definite problem would arise—despite the fact that they had a written agreement or contract. The court probably would not hold the young girl to that agreement and would probably stake out for her a new claim— maybe equal to his. She would be deemed to have been the victim of fraud, lack of understanding, undue influence, or possibly all three.

The written contract would be unfair by its terms. It was inequitable and not at arm's length to begin with. A contract means a fair but not necessarily an equal exchange of value. The worldly lawyer would presumably have been to bed with the girl of the hills before she moved in with him, and she would have been taken to dinner at some place like the Playboy Club or to a Hollywood disco. The lawyer would have influenced her greatly. Also the fact that he was a lawyer, himself—thus violating that cardinal bit of wisdom, "he who has himself for a lawyer usually has a fool for a client"—and that she had only the wisdom of her seventeen summers in the mountains would be a distinct disadvantage for the girl.

Maybe this example is not so far-fetched. A goodly number of young girls not much older than our mountain flower and not necessarily much more sophisticated go off to Los Angeles, Chicago and New York and all points in between and eventually move in with older, wiser and wealthier men.

Problems can also arise with a written document if it was signed under duress, due to threats or through fraud. A contract is not valid if one person signed it with a literal or even figurative gun to his or her head.

If Dick and Jane have come to a parting of the ways, and Dick sticks a written agreement in front of her and says, "You sign this paper or I won't let you out of the apartment" (alive, being the implication), you have a classic case of obvious duress.

Or, let's say Dick presents Jane with an agreement before they move in together. "Look," he says, "just sign this agreement. Don't worry—I'm not going to hold you to it. It's only to appease my business manager. I'll tear it up one month from today. Just move in and take care of the apartment and type my novel and cook for me." If Jane moved in and did all these things and then in a month Dick refused to tear up the agreement, you probably have undue influence, fraud, or an equally effective defense.

But if you have a fair, "arm's length" agreement which both the mountain girl and her man entered into without undue influence or taking advantage, and with clear understanding as to its terms and what was being bargained for, then the agreement will probably stand up.

Sometimes a person enters into an agreement with all the proper safeguards, but then does a great deal more than what was agreed to. Jane agreed to do the cooking, but then she provided not merely adequate meals but elaborate, gourmet French and Italian delights. Jane may then say she's entitled to more because of these extras, but she will probably be held to the benefits of the bargain that was struck. On the other hand, if she had no agreement and did more than an ordinary mate would do, Jane might get more in a legal battle under doctrines of equitable remedies and fair treatment.

If there is a written agreement and it is fair, the parties no doubt will be held to it. If there is no written agreement, then the cohabitant who wants something out of the broken relationship must prove that there is an express oral agreement capable of fair and meaningful interpretation or an implied agreement, or some other basis for relief.

The person—usually the woman—who asserts the agreement has the burden of proof to convince the court by the preponderance of the evidence that such an agreement took place. The problem, of course, is that many times these oral agreements are made during what are regarded as "pillow talk" conversations when there are no witnesses. They are made under circumstances of love and emotion—as part of a "confidential relationship"—and there is always the question of what was really meant. Pillow talk promises are often vague, ambiguous and hard to pin down. What does it mean when he says, "Stick with me, baby, I'll take care of you"? Probably not much, unfortunately, for the one asserting the agreement.

In live-in arrangements where there is no written agreement, actions may speak louder than words. In the absence of something in writing—or if one of the parties denies there was an oral agreement—then you must try to prove an "implied" agreement. How do you do that? There are several ways.

First, some witnesses would be helpful. Of course, the witnesses would not have been in the bedroom during that pillow talk. Still, they know something about how Dick and Jane lived. The couple who live across the hall or down the block, social friends who went to the same parties, coworkers and relatives—all or any of them can shed light on the relationship.

"Oh, they were such a loving couple," such a witness might be able to testify. "They acted like a married couple. Dick was always talking about 'our home' and 'our life.' He was always buying her clothes for her—he wouldn't let her pick out a thing."

A showing that a couple acted toward each other in a loving way indicates an inclination to share a life, and, by implication, share property, too.

Jane might claim the implied agreement was shown by the fact that they had a joint checking account; and sure enough, the checkbook deposits show they both put money into the same account. That gives evidence of an agreement to share.

If the couple buy property together, that is another piece of evidence—and a strong one.

Let us take another example. Let us say a man tells his "friend," "Go look for a house for us." She goes out and looks at houses for six months, and finally finds something she likes. Dick looks at it and says, "Okay, I like it." If they buy that house and move in together, that sequence of actions indicates a desire on Dick's part to share at least the house with Jane.

Maybe he says, "Let's build a house." She does the decorating and works closely with the builder. They plan rooms specifically with her in mind. They design and install mirrors that are fixed at the level of five feet three—her height. These things indicate some sort of sharing—that the house was meant to be shared. It is the way you live that can by implication show you agree to share with your unmarried spouse something more than just your time.

The fact is that the better a man treats a woman he is living with, the more indication there is that he meant to share property with her. It raises her "reasonable expectations," a concept the California Supreme Court has declared could be a predicate for enforcing a contract action. All these situations are relative, of course. Each case depends upon how much property and assets are involved and when they were accumulated. The property and assets susceptible to being shared are the property and assets accumulated by the couple during the time they are together. What each party brings to the relationship separately usually remains separate, but may get thrown into the common pot as a result of overexpansive behavior on the part of one or the other of the partners.

A compelling conclusion at this stage of the law's development would be that both of the live-togethers are certainly better off if they can agree between themselves how to divide up whatever property they have accumulated during the time they have been together, rather than leaving it up to a court or jury to decide.

Sam and Sally are a young couple who are both working; Sam brings with him to the relationship his stereo and his records, and Sally brings her dishes and books. Together they buy a double bed, two chairs and two lamps. If they can agree that one will take the bed and the other one the two lamps and chairs, they have saved themselves a headache. If they have bought a car together, or a house, or there is a bank account to which they have both contributed and they cannot agree who should get what, then a judge might have to decide. If there is a fair written agreement, all is well. If there is no written agreement but they agree orally, all is well. If there is a dispute over a written agreement or a denial by either party that there was an oral or an implied agreement, all is not well—proving again the old adage, all's fair in love and war. It could all end up before a judge or a jury, who would have to decide what is fair for both parties.

Although live-together agreements are basically to limit the liability of one or both of the partners, they may also contain provisions to share. This could be especially necessary if one of the parties is a nonworking spouse totally dependent upon the other. As we have seen, a young couple both of whom work and who have little or no property may want an agreement that establishes no strings.

Let us consider an agreement in which the woman is a nonworking homemaker. Here, the agreement is that the parties will share the man's earnings equally, and will also share expenses equally. The consideration is the woman's companionship and homemaking.

The woman will, of course, pay her half of the living expenses —food, clothing, essentials—out of the money given to her by the man. Whatever each has left over after contributing equally for living expenses remains his or hers. Also, it is agreed that the woman will keep as her own any money she makes doing extra work. Maybe, for instance, she teaches piano in her spare time.

Because a couple "holding themselves out" as married, or applying for joint credit, tend to show that they plan to share their property, the agreement states that although Mary may use John's name and they might obtain joint credit, these actions are not to be taken to imply any such intention.

In the financial statements at the end of this sample agreement, the man and the woman have listed the real and personal property they wish to protect as their separate property. The woman has moved in with the man on his cattle ranch. Among the property she brought with her that she wishes to have separately protected, she lists her piano, her car and her silverware. The man lists his ranch, his house, cattle, stock truck, furnishings and life insurance.

NONMARITAL PARTNERSHIP
AGREEMENT

THIS AGREEMENT is between MARY SMITH (hereinafter "MARY") and JOHN DOE (hereinafter "JOHN"). This Agreement shall be effective retroactively from _____.

RECITALS

This Agreement is made with reference to the following facts:
1. The parties began living together in _____.
2. They are currently living together and contemplate continuing to do so in the future.
3. The parties desire to define their financial rights and responsibilities, insofar as these can be foreseen.
4. John is a cattle rancher and Mary is a homemaker.
5. The parties currently live in a residence at _____
_____.

NOW, THEREFORE, IN CONSIDERATION of the mutual promises contained herein, the parties agree as follows:
1. *Present Financial Position*
Both parties acknowledge that they have been furnished balance sheets by the other party which set forth financial information concerning their present financial condition.
Each party represents to the other that he or she has fully disclosed to the other his or her financial situation by the representations contained in the balance sheets subject only to the covenant that the balance sheets were prepared informally and without reference to documentation.
2. *Assets and Liabilities as Separate Property of the Parties*
Each of the parties agrees that the property described hereafter is and shall remain the separate property of the party in whom title is held:
    a. All property whether realty or personally owned by either party as of _____.
    b. All property acquired hereafter by either party out of the proceeds or income from property he or she owned as of or attributable to appreciation in value of said property,

whether the enhancement is due to market conditions or to the services, skills or efforts of either of the parties.

c. All property hereafter acquired by either party by gift, devise or inheritance.

3. *Earnings of John*

The parties mutually agree that while they are living together, Mary will be entitled to one-half of all earnings which John accumulates resulting from his personal services, skill, efforts and work and one-half of all property acquired or income derived therefrom.

4. *Earnings of Mary*

The parties mutually agree that while they are living together, the earnings and accumulations resulting from Mary's personal services, skill, efforts and work, together with all property acquired or income derived therefrom, shall be and remain her separate property.

5. *Living Expenses of the Parties*

The parties mutually agree that each person shall contribute, on a monthly basis, one-half of the funds required for living expenses. To the extent that either party is unable to make a required contribution, no indebtedness shall accrue.

6. *Dispositions of Property to Other Party*

Notwithstanding any other provision of this Agreement, either party may, by appropriate written instrument only, transfer, convey, devise or bequeath any property to the other. Neither party intends by this Agreement to limit or restrict in any way the right to receive any such transfer, conveyance, devise or bequest from the other, except as herein stated.

7. *Consideration for Agreement*

The consideration for this Agreement is the mutual promise of each party to contribute the support of the other. In consideration of JOHN's promise to give one-half of his earnings to MARY, she additionally promises to act as companion and homemaker to him.

8. It is agreed between the parties that any services which either party may provide to the other or for the benefit of the other are fully compensated by the consideration paragraph 7, *supra*.

9. *Use of Name*

The parties hereby agree that Mary shall have the right to use the name DOE and to hold herself out as JOHN's spouse. However, this shall not affect the rights of the parties as set forth in this Agreement nor shall the applications for joint credit affect any financial arrangements set forth herein.

10. *Integration.*

This Agreement sets forth the entire agreement between the parties with regard to the subject matter hereof. All agreements, covenants, representations and warranties, express and implied, oral and written, of the parties with regard to their financial relationship, past, present and future, commencing as of the date they began living together and terminating if and when they separate, are contained herein. No other agreements, covenants, representations, or warranties, express or implied, oral or written, have been made by either party to the other with respect to the subject matter of this Agreement. All prior and contemporaneous conversations, negotiations, possible and alleged agreements and representations, covenants and warranties with respect to the subject matter hereof are waived, merged herein and superseded hereby. This is an integrated agreement.

11. *Amendment*

As set forth in Civil Code §1698, this Agreement can be amended only by a written agreement signed by both parties or an executed oral agreement.

12. *Governing Law*

This Agreement has been drafted and executed in _____ _____ and shall be governed by, continued and enforced in accordance with the laws of the State of _____.

13. *Severability*

In the event any of the provisions of this Agreement are deemed to be invalid or unenforceable, the same shall be deemed serverable from the remainder of this Agreement and shall not cause the invalidity or unenforceability of the remainder of this Agreement.

14. *Signing the Agreement*

Prior to signing this Agreement, each party consulted with an attorney of his or her choice and the terms and legal significance of the foregoing Agreement and the effect which it has upon any interest which each party might accrue in the property of the other were fully explained. Each party acknowledges that he or she fully understands the foregoing Agreement and its legal effect, and that he or she is signing the same freely and voluntarily and that neither party has any reason to believe that the other did not understand fully the terms and effects of the Agreement or that he or she did not freely and voluntarily execute said Agreement.

15. *Costs and Expenses*

Each party hereto shall bear his or her respective costs and expenses incurred in connection with this Agreement, including without limitation the negotiation, preparation and consummation thereof.

16. *Captions*

Paragraph titles or captions contained herein are inserted as a matter of convenience and for reference and in no way define, limit, extend or describe the scope of this Agreement or any provision hereof.

17. *Interpretation*

No provision in this Agreement is to be interpreted for or against any party because that party or that party's legal representative drafted the provision.

18. *Attorneys' Fees*

Should any party hereto retain counsel for the purpose of enforcing or preventing the breach of any provision hereof, by instituting any action or proceeding to enforce any provision hereof, for damages by reason of any alleged breach of any provision hereof, for a declaration of such party's rights or obligations hereunder or for any other judicial remedy, then the prevailing party shall be entitled to be reimbursed by the losing party for all costs and expenses incurred thereby, including, but not limited to, reasonable attorneys' fees and costs for the services rendered to such prevailing party.

19. *Execution in Counterparts*

This Agreement may be executed in two or more counterparts, each of which shall be an original but all of which shall constitute one and the same instrument.

IN WITNESS WHEREOF, this Agreement is signed this ____
day of _____, _____, at _____.

MARY SMITH

JOHN DOE

ATTORNEYS' CERTIFICATIONS

The undersigned hereby certifies that he is an attorney at law,
duly licensed to practice in the State of _____; that he has
been employed by JOHN DOE, one of the parties to the foregoing Nonmarital Partnership Agreement; that he has advised and
consulted with JOHN DOE with respect to his and MARY
SMITH's rights and has fully explained to him the legal significance of the foregoing Nonmarital Partnership Agreement and
the effect which it has upon his rights otherwise obtaining as a
matter of law; that JOHN DOE, after being fully advised by the
undersigned, acknowledged to the undersigned that he understood fully the terms of the foregoing Nonmarital Partnership
Agreement and the legal effect thereof, and that he had executed
the same freely and voluntarily; and that the undersigned has no
reason to believe that JOHN DOE did not understand fully such
terms and effects or that he did not freely and voluntarily execute
said Agreement, such execution being in the undersigned's presence.

Dated: _____, _____

The undersigned hereby certifies that he is an attorney at law,
duly licensed to practice in the State of _____; that he has
been employed by MARY SMITH, one of the parties to the foregoing Nonmarital Partnership Agreement; that he has advised
and consulted with MARY SMITH with respect to her and JOHN
DOE's rights and has fully explained to her the legal significance
of the foregoing Nonmarital Partnership Agreement and the effect
which it has upon her rights otherwise obtaining as a matter of

law; that MARY SMITH, after being fully advised by the undersigned, acknowledged to the undersigned that she understood fully the terms of the foregoing Nonmarital Partnership Agreement and the legal effect thereof, and that she had executed the same freely and voluntarily; and that the undersigned has no reason to believe that MARY SMITH did not understand fully such terms and effects or that she did not freely and voluntarily execute said Agreement, such execution being in the undersigned's presence.

Dated: _____, _____

JOHN'S FINANCIAL STATEMENT
ASSETS AND LIABILITIES TO
REMAIN AS SEPARATE PROPERTY

Cash—$5,000
J. & D. Ranch, Cimarron County, State. Approx. 340 acres
      Book value—$75,000
      Loan on property—$23,500
Ranch house on J. & D. Ranch
      Book value—$46,000
      Loan—$8,500
Furniture and furnishings in ranch house
1980 Ford truck: state license number JD-100
Livestock and cattle: approx. 150 head; approx. value, $10,000
Cattleman's Life Insurance policy: face value, $50,000

MARY'S FINANCIAL STATEMENT
ASSETS AND LIABILITIES TO
REMAIN AS SEPARATE PROPERTY

Cash—$1,500
Wurlitzer spinet piano
1979 Chevrolet Monte Carlo: state license number MS-2
Sterling silver flatware service for eight
Clothing, jewelry and personal effects
Life insurance policy: face value, $8,000

4

ONCE BITTEN,
TWICE SHY

THERE MAY NOT BE a more explosive word among the disaffected legion of the divorced than *alimony,* that persistent, bitter aftertaste of a marriage gone sour. But if the payment of alimony to an ex-wife (or husband) causes emotional dynamite for a divorced man (or woman), paying alimony to an ex who has moved in with a new lover carries with it the destructive power of emotional TNT. And yet, in a disintegrating social system peopled more and more by divorced or separated persons, it is inevitable that many of the formerly marrieds will drift into the ranks of the unmarried cohabitants.

What happens when a husband who is paying his ex-wife $500-a-month alimony discovers that she has moved in with another man? If she married the man, the first husband's $500-a-month alimony payments would stop. But if she only lives with the man, he may have to continue to pay.

In earlier, less complicated days, such situations were crystal clear in the eyes of the law. An ex-wife who went off and lived with another man without marriage was a brazen hussy in the same general class as a meretricious spouse, that is, a prostitute. She deserved the same treatment.

As the court declared in *Weber* v. *Weber*, a 1913 Wisconsin case cited by J. Thomas Oldham in a 1978–79 family-law article in the *University of Louisville Law School Journal:* "If the wife, without the fault of the husband, and without any adequate excuse of palliation, deliberately chooses a life of shame and dishonor . . . the court may make the misconduct of the wife the ground for cutting off all alimony. . . . the courts of our state do not permit vice to flaunt its banner before them unchallenged."

Traditionally, separation or divorce decrees provided that alimony would continue to be paid to the ex-spouse until the "death or remarriage" of the recipient. (Child support, which is separate, is paid usually until the child is eighteen, depending upon the decree and the jurisdiction. Child-support payments, of course, are not affected by remarriage or cohabitation of the other parent.)

Even though making alimony payable until "death or remarriage" sounds like a lifetime sentence, alimony awards may be later modified by the court if there is a significant "change in circumstances" and if such awards have not been made "nonmodifiable" by agreement of the parties to begin with. If the man who is paying loses his job, for example, or becomes physically disabled so as to impair his ability to pay, the terms could be modified. If the woman's economic situation improved greatly, thus decreasing her need for support from him, the alimony could be reduced, too.

In the less sexually permissive days of *Weber* v. *Weber,* the courts did not seem to consider it necessary to suggest that alimony would terminate in case of a divorced spouse "living in sin." The swift alimony termination for the wife who apparently had enlisted under a "banner of vice" makes it clear the omission did not mean that cohabitation was acceptable. On the contrary, the ruling leaves no doubt that "living in sin" was such an obvious condition for termination of alimony as not even to require stating.

More recently, a divorced woman receiving alimony and cohabiting with a man might find herself to be part of a "de facto" marriage—a family-style relationship that has all the elements of a marriage except a marriage license. Or if she lived in a common-law-marriage state, she might be declared married under the common law. In either case, she could find her alimony terminated.

But, in today's revolutionary social climate, "living in sin" is no longer looked upon as unspeakable or even legally considered to be "a life of shame and dishonor."

As the California Supreme Court has said, "The mores of the society have indeed changed so radically in regard to cohabitation that we cannot impose a standard based on alleged moral considerations that have apparently been so widely abandoned by so many."

Some observers have declared that there now exists a new category that could be termed "legal meretricious cohabitation," a condition that is not quite marriage, yet is legally recognized.

It remains to be seen how far the law may eventually go in recognizing these various relationships, but a couple who live together with a written agreement, an express oral agreement or an implied agreement have legal standing and legal remedies. Legal marriage, de facto marriage, common-law marriage and cohabitation are now categories to be reckoned with. And if a man's ex-wife who is collecting alimony goes off and lives with another man, what then? May the ex-husband terminate alimony or does he have to keep on paying to support his ex when she's living with another guy?

Reaction to the *Marvin* v. *Marvin* case brought about a split in legal viewpoints. One view, as embodied in a 1977 New York statute, holds that the court may terminate alimony if the supported party is cohabiting with a person of the opposite sex and they are "holding themselves out" as husband and wife. The other viewpoint, embodied in a 1978 California statute, holds that a divorced or separated spouse cohabiting with another partner of the opposite sex is presumed to have diminished need for support. Upon such a finding of "changed circumstances," a judge may modify the alimony payments.

In other words, in New York State and some other states, a man who discovers his wife is living with a man can go to court and get his alimony payments terminated. In California and some other states, a man paying alimony may be able to get the payments reduced, or maybe even suspended for as long as the former wife continues to live with a man. If they separate and he or she moves out, he may have to resume paying alimony.

The view that alimony should be terminated if an ex takes up with another partner seems to be a mixture of punitive sexual outrage and the contention that the new partner can and should support the ex-spouse. The other view seems to be morally neutral and considers only whether the "changed circumstances" of the new cohabitation require a modification of the alimony. From either view, the courts are presented with an extension of the traditional posture that alimony is to be paid only until the "death or remarriage" of the alimony recipient.

Faced with such situations, the courts have responded in different ways. In New York, courts have terminated alimony where an ex-wife was living with another man and the couple were "holding themselves out as husband and wife." That amounted to a "de facto marriage" and fell under the general view that alimony shall terminate upon the remarriage of the alimony recipient. In an Ohio case, a judge terminated alimony to an ex-wife on grounds that the woman, who was living with another man, was a party to a common-law marriage. In that case, *Fahrer* v. *Fahrer*, the woman had moved out of Ohio, where common-law marriage is recognized, into a state where it was not recognized. But the court still declared that she was, in fact, married under the common law as far as Ohio was concerned, because if she were still living in Ohio she would be part of a common-law marriage.

Both of these rulings are in line with the traditional public policy to encourage marriage and discourage divorce. They also view cohabitation from the vantage point of the "wronged" alimony payer and not from the point of view of the support needs of the alimony recipient.

The reasoning behind such rulings, as indicated, is based partly on the contention that the new partner in the ex-spouse's life should support the person. In most cases, however, the new partner takes the position that he is not supporting the woman and is not interested in taking up such a burden. The argument is usually to the effect that, "I'm supporting myself; she's supporting herself. It's fifty-fifty but separate."

In some cases, of course, the new partner cannot support the woman, either because he does not have sufficient income or because he is, in turn, paying alimony and/or child support for *his* ex-wife. Such are the entanglements that can arise in our new so-called permissive society.

It is interesting to note that both the California and New York statutes describe unmarried cohabitation between persons "of the opposite sex." And yet a 1978 Minnesota case concerned two members of the same sex.

That case, *Anonymous* v. *Anonymous*, involved a couple who separated and the man was ordered to pay his estranged wife alimony. She afterward professed to be a Lesbian and established a live-in relationship with another Lesbian. The estranged husband sought to halt alimony on the grounds that this constituted a "change in circumstances," and the court so ruled.

The New York and California statutes as drafted, requiring cohabitation by "persons of the opposite sex," would seem not to extend to homosexuals.

Usually, the new partner contributes something to the alimony recipient's support gratuitously, and that, too, can be considered a "change in circumstances" which could result in lowered alimony payments. If that cohabitant later halts the gratuitous support, the former husband could have to resume paying full alimony.

Sometimes, too, the new partner could support the woman but will not if he is not legally obligated to.

A fascinating example of this, and a look at how California handles such cases, is afforded by the 1978 reported case, *In re Marriage of Leib*. Mr. and Mrs. Leib were divorced after a fifteen-year marriage, and she received $500 a month alimony. While continuing to get support, she moved in with Leonard Elbaum, who earned $30,000 a year, owned a $90,000 house and had two Ferraris. Mrs. Leib herself drove a Ferrari, traveled to Europe for six weeks and at the time the case reached the court of appeal had $50,000 in savings accounts. She had been living with Elbaum for more than two years at that time.

Elbaum said he did not support Mrs. Leib, but evidence

showed he contributed $2,000 a month toward support of her and her child. She fulfilled the role of housewife, but was not paid for such services.

The court of appeal decided that Mrs. Leib was enabled to "give away" her services as homemaker to Elbaum because of the fact that she was collecting $500 a month in alimony from her ex-husband. Thus, Mr. Leib was, in effect, subsidizing Elbaum and the relationship.

Oldham, a legal scholar and a member of the *U.C.L.A. Law Review*, noted in his law journal article on the case: "The court said that, in any event, it was unfair for her to 'contribute her services' as a housewife to the new household and not receive compensation. The court emphasized that her services as a homemaker, housekeeper, cook and companion had a significant value, a principle that was established by the earlier Marvin Supreme Court decision.

"The court held that 'she had no right . . . to collect . . . from her former husband spousal support in a sum . . . sufficient to enable her to make a gift of such services,' and that an alimony recipient 'cannot give away his or her services where the result is to create a status of apparent continuing need for alimony.' The court did not attempt to place a value upon the services contributed by the alimony recipient: it merely held that the $500 monthly alimony should be reduced to a token amount while the cohabitation continued."

The effect was that Mr. Leib's alimony payments of $500 a month were reduced to the token amount of $10 a month for as long as Mrs. Leib lived with Elbaum.

The Leib case suggests that in California, at least, a divorced woman who moves in with another man and fulfills the role of housewife will find her alimony suspended or reduced to a token payment.

Oldham comments: "The court seems piqued that an alimony recipient can cohabit with another solvent person and continue to receive alimony. But isn't this what must follow from a judicial acknowledgment of informal relationships and different levels of commitment?"

How to deal with this more and more pervasive problem will continue to be a perplexing question. "Terminating or even suspending alimony automatically upon unmarried cohabitation by a recipient would be unfair and unjustified,'' Oldham comments.

The dilemma concerns whether the view is to be that Pontius Pilate washes his hands of any divorced woman or man who goes off and lives in sin with another and is subsidized by the unfortunate alimony payer, or whether the question to be considered is where support for the alimony recipient is to come from. The first view stems from the Puritan past and the second from the public-policy approach that the alimony recipient should not wind up on the welfare lists.

Whereas one view would modify or suspend alimony if an ex lives in sin, the other—or at least the New York statute—would terminate alimony if the spouse and her/his new partner ''hold themselves out'' as husband and wife, thus creating a ''de facto marriage'' and releasing the alimony payer.

The result of these policies is that various ex-wives ''living in sin'' simply do not ''hold themselves out'' as married, but keep their own names, maintain separate bank accounts and insist they are not being supported by their new partners. If they married, the alimony would be lost. Thus, such policies sometimes have the effect of keeping couples ''living in sin'' rather than getting married to avoid losing alimony. This brings about the opposite result than the one sought—to encourage marriage.

In the Ohio case of *Fahrer* v. *Fahrer,* for instance, the divorced wife testified in a sworn deposition that the reason she had not remarried was that she didn't want to lose the alimony. Living in sin, she could keep it. It is the same problem encountered by many elderly widows who face the loss of their husbands' Social Security benefits if they remarry.

The widespread existence of ''de facto'' marriages and cohabitation not only results in wives who receive alimony while living with other men, but it goes a step further. Because ''palimony'' decisions have resulted in unmarried cohabitants being directed to pay alimony to spouses they never married, the situation is created where an unmarried woman who is collecting ''alimony'' is living with another new partner—still without marrying. Should an unmarried man pay ''alimony'' to a woman he never married while she's living with another man? This is not merely a fanciful exercise in supposition, because the case law has now established the precedent that an unmarried man may be directed to pay alimony or rehabilitative support to a woman he never married. If she then moves in with another paramour— what then? Consider, for example, the 1979 Kozlowski case in New Jersey.

In 1962, Irma Kozlowski, forty-eight, a married woman with two children, moved in with Thaddeus Kozlowski, then forty-two, who also was married and had two children. Irma, a Polish immigrant who barely spoke English, was married to a man with the same name as her new partner. There could be no question of a "de facto" marriage here, because both were already married. It was clearly a relationship in which neither could expect to marry the other.

Six years later, Mrs. Kozlowski divorced her husband and moved out of Koslowski's home in Smoke Rise, New Jersey. But Thaddeus, a wealthy businessman, prevailed upon her to move back in, promising to take care of her for the rest of her life. He was still married.

In 1977, after fifteen years together, Thaddeus finally divorced his first wife, left Irma and married another woman. Irma sued, citing the Marvin decision, and insisted that an express agreement existed. Thaddeus fought the case, arguing that if a contract did exist it was invalid because one or both of them was married during the entire fifteen years, and that made their relationship adulterous.

The New Jersey Supreme Court in a 7–0 decision upheld a superior court trial ruling that Irma was entitled to support for the rest of her life. An amount of $55,000 was awarded, to be paid to Irma based upon her remaining years of life expectancy and prorated upon the amount she received during her years with Kozlowski.

The court could find neither de facto marriage nor common-law marriage, because common law is not recognized in New Jersey. "To dispel any misunderstanding, we emphasize that our decision today has not judicially revived a form of common-law marriage, which has been proscribed in New Jersey since 1939," the Supreme Court declared. "We do no more than recognize that society's mores have changed and that an agreement between adult parties living together is enforceable to the extent that it is not based on a relationship proscribed by law or on a promise to marry.''

Kozlowski is the kind of result that may be expected in the twenty-four states that have accepted express or implied contracts between unmarried persons.

In another case, in Buffalo, New York, a trial court granted alimony to a woman who had lived with a man in an unmarried state for twenty-eight years and borne a child. In that case, *McCullon* v. *McCullon,* the court found that an implied agreement existed. Because they had lived together as husband and wife for twenty-eight years and the woman had provided wifely services and companionship, it was implied that he would support her for the rest of her life if they separated, the court decided.

The court apparently was not too comfortable with that reasoning, however, because it buttressed its decision by also finding that the couple had formed a common-law marriage—this in a state that does not recognize common-law marriage. It solved that problem by finding that the couple had vacationed in Pennsylvania, where common-law marriage is recognized, and therefore they had created a common-law marriage under Pennsylvania law.

An intriguing question is raised by such cases. What if a woman in such a case—of the Kozlowski or McCullon type, both of whom are receiving continuing alimony—moves in with a new partner? Presumably, if she did, that would reflect a ''change of condition'' and the alimony could be terminated, suspended or reduced in the same manner as though she were divorced from a legal marriage.

Other variations also exist in this complex, many-sided, new anything-goes society. The California community-property law, the California no-fault statute and case law can combine to create a tangled economic mess as demonstrated by a situation that was known in California as ''the captain's paradise'' case. The original captain's-paradise story concerned a ship's captain who had wives in each of the two ports to which he sailed. In California, the central figure was Santa Barbara eye surgeon Richard Baragry, who lived with his wife, Barbara, and their two daughters in domestic bliss until August 4, 1971. Then came an angry quarrel, and Dr. Baragry stormed out of the house. He took up residence on his boat.

Sometime thereafter, the doctor rented an apartment and moved into it with Karen Lucien, twenty-eight, who had worked for him as a secretary.

But the doctor, apparently nagged by what he called his "solid midwestern upbringing," was reluctant to divorce his wife. Instead, he often went home for dinner and then later went to his apartment to spend the night with Ms. Lucien. Mrs. Baragry, also reluctant to break up the marriage, kept hoping that her husband would see the light and move back home, and so she allowed him to continue dining at home.

During the rest of 1971 and all during 1972, the doctor had dinner at home almost every night, and after that he had dinner at home three to five times a week. He paid all the household bills as usual, supported his family and filed joint income-tax returns with his wife. He received his mail at home, and it was his voting address as well. He also brought his laundry home twice a month for his wife to wash and iron.

During all this time, he was spending his nights at the apartment with Ms. Lucien. And during this time, according to the testimony of both the doctor and his wife, there was no sex between them.

The Baragrys thus maintained an outwardly middle-class appearance as a typical married couple. Dr. Baragry sent his wife Christmas, birthday and anniversary cards, plus gifts, and took her to social and professional events such as dinners at the houses of other doctors and friends, dinners of professional and academic groups and outings with fellow physicians. He took his wife and daughters on vacation trips to Yosemite and San Francisco in 1971 and 1972 and regularly to basketball games at the University of California at Santa Barbara. In 1973, he took his wife to Sun Valley for a week without the children. On Christmas Eve, 1971, he slept at home. In 1974, he filed an enrollment card for his daughter at a private school stating that she lived at home with both her parents.

The doctor was still married to Mrs. Baragry, but he had sex only with Ms. Lucien in their apartment. This went on for four years, with the wife hoping that her husband would resume their marriage.

But on October 14, 1975, the doctor finally filed for divorce, declaring that he and Mrs. Baragry had been separated and living apart since August of 1971 when he had moved in with Ms. Lucien.

That is when the captain's paradise started turning into the captain's mast—this time for the captain.

Mrs. Baragry insisted that the doctor had moved out and they had separated only on October 14, 1975, when he actually filed divorce papers. She demanded her half of their community property for the four years between August of 1971 and October of 1975.

The Santa Barbara Superior Court ruled that the doctor was correct that the marriage had ended in 1971; but the court of appeal reversed and said the later date, 1975, prevailed.

"The question is whether the parties' conduct evidences a complete and final break in the marital relationship," the court noted. "Here the only evidence of such a break is the absence of an active sexual relationship between the parties and husband's cohabitation elsewhere with a girlfriend. In our view such evidence is not tantamount to legal separation."

It went on: "Husband was presumably enjoying a captain's paradise, savoring the best of two worlds and capturing the benefits of both. Wife was furnishing all the normal wifely contributions to a marriage that husband was willing to accept and most of the services normally furnished in a twenty-year-old marriage. Husband was reaping the advantages of those services and may be presumed to owe part of his professional success during that four-year period to wife's social and domestic efforts on his behalf.

"One who enjoys the benefit of a polygamous life-style must be prepared to accept its accompanying financial burdens," the court declared.

In conclusion, it said: "To hold otherwise would be tantamount to saying that because husband slept on the living room couch for four years, or because he regularly slept elsewhere with another woman, wife can be deprived of her share in the household earnings."

In such a case, under the California community-property law, the wife would be entitled to half of the doctor's property and earnings. The intriguing question is what would happen if the "other woman" in such a triangle demanded the other half of his property in a palimony suit.

When living in sin may be equated with "de facto" marriage, common-law marriage or "Marvinizing," a man could find himself treated as a bigamist—not criminally but economically.

The new cohabitation life-style has created a situation that we might describe as "divorce without marriage." When enough property is to be divided or when the cohabitation has been long enough to justify support payments upon ending the relationship, written separation agreements may be drawn up. This is, in effect, "bargaining out" of a relationship, as opposed to drawing up a living-together agreement in advance.

These nonmarital separation agreements have no standing in family-law or domestic-relations court, of course. Like nonmarital live-together agreements, they are contract matters pure and simple. Still, they contain essentially the same elements as a court-ordered alimony decree. A nonmarital separation agreement properly drawn up by attorneys, signed by both parties, notarized and filed with the clerk of the civil court that has jurisdiction is as close to a "divorce" as nonmarried couples can come.

Such a separation agreement can contain a modifiable support clause declaring that the support payments will cease if the alimony recipient moves in with a new partner, or gets married. It can also stipulate that the payments will end after either a certain amount of time has passed or after a certain amount of money has been paid. It can contain any agreement clause the two parties feel is necessary.

For example, if a couple have lived together for four years while Tom attended college and Sally worked, a separation agreement could declare that Tom will pay support to Sally at so much per month until she finishes college.

Of course, the agreement might also state that Tom's support payments to Sally will *not* halt if she moves in with a new partner. That would be an agreement with a nonmodifiable support clause.

One might wonder under what circumstances a partner who is unmarried would be willing to agree to support another person after they are no longer living together. Probably young people who have been together only a short time and who own very little would not fall into this category, but couples who have been together for many years are in a different situation. In many such cases, the woman has stayed home and is totally dependent upon the male wage earner, unable to go back out into the job market. In a typical case, the man realizes that if the woman goes to court in a "palimony" action he may be found liable and will be ordered to pay. A voluntary separation agreement may then seem preferable, and could save money in the long run.

Here is an example of a separation agreement involving unmarried cohabitants. It includes a support clause that may be made modifiable or nonmodifiable.

Let us assume here that the couple have been together long enough to decide to split things down the middle. Although a couple working up an agreement in advance might not list the value of every piece of property, it can become a different ball game when they make a division of property upon splitting up. Dividing equally means each gets half of the value, so they must first establish and agree upon the total value of their accumulated property. After the division, each must have an equal amount.

In this example, the woman takes the house as her major piece of property, and the man takes the hardware store. The rest is parceled out until each has a fair portion.

In addition, the man agrees to pay his former partner $600-a-month support for five years. During that time, she agrees to try to find a way to support herself. As Mary begins to earn money, the amount John must pay her will be reduced by an equal amount. When Mary begins making $200 a month, John will only have to pay her the difference to make up the $600—or $400. John agrees to make up the difference up to $600 each month for five years, after which time his obligation ceases.

SEPARATION AGREEMENT

THIS SEPARATION AGREEMENT is made and entered into this ____ day of _____, 19___, by and between

_____, hereinafter referred to as "JOHN" and _____, hereinafter referred to as "MARY" with reference to the following facts:

WHEREAS the parties hereto began living together on _____, 19____, in the City of _____, County of _____, State of _____; and

WHEREAS, the parties presently reside at _____ _____ which falls in the geographical boundaries of the City of _____ in the State of _____; and

WHEREAS in consequence of unhappy differences and irreconcilable disputes which have arisen between JOHN and MARY, as a result of which they have ceased to reside together and are considering living separate and apart during the remainder of their lives; and

WHEREAS, it is the mutual wish of both JOHN and MARY to immediately effect a settlement of their respective property rights and to provide for MARY's support.

NOW, therefore, by reason of the foregoing facts, it is mutually agreed by and between the parties hereto, as follows:

First: The parties hereto agree that JOHN is possessed of the following property all of which is JOHN's separate property, and MARY does hereby waive any and all right which she may have, if any, in or to the following items of property:

JOHN's financial statement attached as Schedule A.

Second: The parties hereto agree that MARY is possessed of the following property, which is MARY's separate property, and JOHN does hereby waive any and all right which he may have, if any, in or to all of the following property:

MARY's financial statement attached as Schedule B.

Third: JOHN agrees to pay MARY for her support and maintenance the sum of $600.00 per month, commencing on the first day of January, 1981, and continuing thereafter up to and including December 31, 1985, or until MARY dies, JOHN dies, MARY gets married, MARY cohabits with an unrelated adult male, whichever should occur first. During the said five year period, said support payments shall not be subject to modification, but shall be subject to earlier termination, as set forth hereinabove and adjustment as provided herein below. MARY acknowledges that she has an obligation to seek and obtain employment and to receive income during the said five year period and, any and all income earned by MARY during the said five year period, regardless of when received, shall be credited against the support payments made by JOHN. MARY shall furnish JOHN, in writing, on or before the first day of each calendar quarter commencing with January 1, 1981, with the amount of gross income earned by MARY in the immediately preceding "calendar" quarter. Said amount earned shall then be offset against future support payments until the full amount earned by MARY has been offset against support payments due her from JOHN.

At the completion of the five year period referred to in this paragraph, unless terminated earlier, as provided for herein, JOHN's obligation to support MARY shall absolutely and unequivocally terminate and MARY agrees that she shall have no right to seek, nor shall any court have any jurisdiction to grant MARY additional support subsequent to December 31, 1985.

Fourth: JOHN expressly waives all rights and claims to receive any money or property for his support from MARY at any time. JOHN expressly acknowledges and agrees that as a result of the execution of this agreement he shall have no right to seek any order from any court which would require MARY to pay JOHN any support payments whatsoever.

Fifth: It is understood and agreed between the parties that during the six-month period subsequent to the execution of this agreement they intend to consider, discuss, and possibly attempt a reconciliation. Accordingly, this agreement shall be valid and binding on JOHN and MARY, their heirs, personal representatives, assigns and other successors of interest, absent a reconciliation between the parties.

Sixth: This agreement, and all of its terms and conditions shall be absolutely binding upon the parties hereto, regardless of whether or not any court approves the contents hereof.

Seventh: JOHN warrants to MARY that he has not incurred and hereby covenants that he will not incur any liabilities or obligations which MARY is or may be liable for, except as expressly set forth herein; and JOHN hereby covenants and agrees that if any claim, action or proceeding shall hereafter be brought seeking to hold MARY liable on account of any debt, liability, act or omission of JOHN, including any obligations incurred by JOHN subsequent to the date of this agreement, he will, at his sole expense, defend MARY against any such claim or demand, whether or not well founded, and that he will hold her free and harmless therefrom.

Eighth: MARY warrants to JOHN that she has not incurred and hereby covenants that she will not incur any liabilities or obligations which JOHN is or may be liable for, except as expressly set forth herein; and MARY hereby covenants and agrees that if any claim, action or proceeding shall hereafter be brought seeking to hold JOHN liable on account of any debt, liability, act or omission of MARY, including any obligations incurred by MARY subsequent to the date of this agreement, she will, at her sole expense, defend JOHN against any such claim or demand, whether or not well founded, and that she will hold him free and harmless therefrom.

Ninth: It is hereby agreed that any and all property acquired by either of the parties to this agreement from and after the date of this agreement is the property of the party acquiring the same, and each of the parties hereto hereby waives any and all right in or to such future acquisitions of property.

Tenth: Each of the parties hereby waives and renounces any and all rights to inherit from the estate of the other at the other's death, or to receive any property of the other under a will executed before the effective date of this agreement, or to claim any family allowance or probate homestead from the other's estate, or to act as executor, to act as administrator, or an administrator with the willingness, of the other's estate, except as the nominee of another person who is legally entitled to make nominations for administrator.

Eleventh: No modification or waiver of any of the terms of this agreement shall be valid as between the parties, unless in writing and executed with the same formality as this agreement; no waiver of any breach or default hereunder shall be deemed as a waiver of any subsequent breach or default of the same or similar nature no matter how made or how often occurring.

Twelfth: Each of the parties agrees, on the demand of the other, to execute any instrument, furnish any information, or perform any other acts and deliver any and all further of the deeds, assignments, insurance forms, papers, or other documents as deemed necessary to carry out the terms of this agreement.

Thirteenth: In the event of a reconciliation between the parties, this agreement shall not continue in full force and effect but shall become void for all purposes.

Fourteenth: Except as otherwise provided for in this agreement, each party has hereby released the other from any and all claims, demands, costs, expenses, liabilities, actions and causes of action of whatsoever kind or nature based on, arising out of, or in connection with any matter, fact or thing occurring on or accruing prior to the date of the execution of this agreement, including all rights and obligations related to their marriage; provided, however, that nothing contained herein or in any of the paragraphs of this agreement shall relieve or discharge either of the parties of and from any of his or her obligations under this agreement or under any other instrument or document executed pursuant to the provisions hereof or related hereto.

Fifteenth: Each party of this agreement hereby stipulates with the other that he or she has been represented in negotiations for and in the preparation of this agreement by counsel of his or her own choosing. Both parties have read this agreement and have had it fully explained to them by their respective counsel. Each of the parties agrees to be responsible for his or her own attorney's fees incurred in connection with this agreement, and with any other action or proceeding related in any manner to their relationship, their rights and obligations attendant thereto, and their rights and obligations under this agreement.

Sixteenth: Each party hereto acknowledges and agrees that he or she is each making this agreement of his or her own respective free will and volition, and acknowledges that no coercion, force, pressure, or undue influence whatsoever has been employed against either party in negotiations leading to the execution of this agreement, either by the other party of this agreement or by any other person or persons whomsoever, and declares that no reliance whatsoever is placed on any representations, other than those expressly set forth herein.

Seventeenth: In the event that any article, paragraph, provision or portion of this agreement shall be held to be invalid, illegal, void or unenforceable, then in such event, the article, paragraph or provision of this agreement held to be invalid, illegal, void or unenforceable, shall be deleted from this agreement, and this agreement shall be read as though such invalid, illegal, void or unenforceable paragraph, provision or portion was never included herein, and the remainder of this agreement shall nevertheless continue in full force and effect.

Eighteenth: The parties agree that the courts of the state of _____ shall have jurisdiction to make such other and further orders that may be necessary to carry out and enforce the terms of this agreement.

MARY acknowledges that she has fully read and has had explained to her all the terms and conditions of this agreement.

JOHN acknowledges that he has fully read and has had explained to him all of the terms and conditions of this agreement.

IN WITNESS WHEREOF, the parties hereto have executed this agreement on the date and year first above written.

_____

JOHN

_____

MARY

APPROVED AS TO FORM BY:

_____

Attorney for JOHN

_____

Attorney for MARY

SCHEDULE A
(JOHN'S ASSETS AND LIABILITIES
AS HIS SEPARATE PROPERTY)

Cash	$7,000.00
Notes receivable	8,000.00
Series E U.S. Savings Bond	1,000.00
19— Chrysler, state license number J-5	6,000.00
John's Hardware Store, 2 Main St	50,000.00
Life Insurance, Liberty Mutual, value	5,000.00
Clothing and personal effects	5,000.00
	$82,000.00

SCHEDULE B
(MARY'S ASSETS AND LIABILITIES
AS HER SEPARATE PROPERTY)

Residence at 10 Splittsville Road	$50,000.00
Furniture and furnishings in house	9,000.00
19— Subaru auto, state license number K-4	6,000.00
Cash	6,000.00
Life insurance policy	7,000.00
Jewelry, clothing, personal effects	4,000.00
	$82,000.00

(Property lists may be considerably more detailed, of course. John's Hardware Store might require a listing of credits and debits, outstanding loans, etc. Mary's house and clothing might require a breakdown, also. The bottom line is that the property going to John equals that going to Mary.)

5

AFTER

THE SPLIT

AFTER SHE HAS THROWN the final plate against the wall and he has put his fist through the partition and it's absolutely, finally, irrevocably over forever—and they really mean it this time—what happens next? He packs his bag and stomps out—or she jumps into the Toyota and vrooms away—and now the unmarried couple's "paper chase" begins. Assuming that two people mutually want to end a live-in relationship, how do they disengage in the most civilized manner?

Naturally, the best solution is to be able to walk away with a minimum of fuss. That means that the two parties agree with each other on the split. She knows what is hers, he knows what is his, and they both agree. Fortunate couple.

But let's say there's a dispute about who owns what.

"That Dylan album is mine!"

"No—the Rolling Stones is yours—Dylan is mine!"

"What does the agreement say?"

So, they dig out a written agreement that listed everything, and there it is, all detailed and neat and precise. Again, there is no problem here. Another fortunate couple.

The problems in a civilized split stem from situations that are not quite so simple or neat and that have not been backed up by a specific, written agreement, which is almost invariably the case. If it were all left to fate and love, and neither quite remembers what was agreed to—or if *anything* was agreed to—and they have been together several years and they have acquired things together, the ingredients are present for anguish. Very often, the first agreement that is reached is the agreement to divide things up when the breakup comes. The natural question is, who gets what?

Generally, under the law, each one gets what he or she brought into the relationship. If he owned a Volkswagen bus when they first hooked up, he still owns it. That stereo of hers which she brought from her old apartment remains hers. And if they can separate everything into things they brought with them when they first moved in together, they, too, should be able to part friends.

The problems, as from the dawn of history, arise with property that both might feel they own. If, in addition to what he brought and what she brought, they put money together and bought a sofa, drapes and a color television set, you have the first possible contretemps. If they kept track of who paid for what and put it in writing, that's great. If they did not but they can agree to some sort of a division—say, he takes the TV and she takes the drapes and sofa—wonderful.

In all such situations, let me declare emphatically, you are far better off if you can settle the division of property between your-selves. In most cases, a simple, even division is probably the easiest solution. Most courts would divide the property that you have accumulated together evenly.

The situations described so far are ordinary and should not present much of a problem unless one of the parties is on a "trip" and wishes to hurt the other one. But let us consider more com-plicated Gordian knots.

Even though the usual rule would be to share what the two accumulate while they are together, there are certainly major exceptions. He may inherit a valuable Rembrandt, which he does not intend to share with her. She may win the Irish Sweepstakes and not include that in their joint accumulation.

They certainly can, if they wish, include such windfalls. They can write out an agreement saying, ''Anything I earn or buy or acquire, I'll share with you,'' and that's different. But generally, without some specific statement of that kind, valuable property acquired separately by one other than through the normal earnings or services rendered during the relationship remains that one's separate property. What is ''theirs'' is what ''they'' both purchase together, or agree to share by express or implied agreement, as the case may be.

If Sally walks in with five Renoirs and shows no evidence that she means to share them with Tom, they remain her separate property. But if she says, ''Tom, come live with me and I'll share my five Renoirs with you, and that's a consideration for our agreement to live together,'' then they are probably half Tom's.

But if Sally says, ''Let's get together and any Renoirs I get from now on we'll share,'' then the five she had to start with are not included. That agreement means, ''I'll share with you from here on in.''

That is, of course, a more likely promise. A millionaire playboy or heiress isn't likely to say, ''Look, you now have half of everything I own.'' He or she is more likely to say, ''Whatever we get together, we'll share.'' There are all different kinds of arrangements, and the difficulty with such arrangements is that the promises are often so vague, so ambiguous, so hard to pin down, that it is difficult to deal with them.

A pillow-talk promise made while making love might seem quite different three years later when one does not wish to give the former love object anything more than the price of a bus trip across town, if that.

The need for a clear agreement—a written agreement—arises more often and usually when the parties involved come into the relationship with substantial property they wish to protect. People who own property, who are high earners, who are likely to acquire more property, are best off—if they don't intend to in any way share their property—to define their intention not to divide their property should a relationship break up. If they wish to make certain that somebody is not going to make a claim for part or half of their property, if they wish to protect their right to acquire property without someone claiming title to it, they had better get something in writing.

Otherwise, that person is liable to find himself or herself the object of a large lawsuit when one-is-company, two's-a-crowd time comes. And that suit could be predicated not upon the other party's intention of taking somebody to the cleaners, or greed, but upon an honest misunderstanding—a belief that one should be rewarded for his or her companionship and support. The person could honestly have assumed that you were going to share your life with her or him, even though that is not quite what you had in mind.

In other words, if you walk into a relationship and you are saying to yourself, ''I don't want to share my property. I make $200,000 a year and I'm going to be buying land and investing,'' you had better have the courage to say so. You had better declare it right out front, because if you do not you are asking for a problem. And by your silence and your subsequent conduct you may richly deserve it.

At any rate, what happens under any of these circumstances when it is over and somebody walks out? What if Susan has been living with Rick for five years and she has no job. She has been staying home, cooking and cleaning, like a good housewife and being a loving companion, and Rick comes home and says, ''So long, kid. I just met a chick at Louie's and I'm going to move in with her.'' In this situation, Susan doesn't even have a job. She has no means of support. She might be in poor health, ready for an emotional breakdown or similarly disadvantaged. She needs help, some temporary support, some means of rehabilitating herself, or at least something to keep her head above water until she can get back into the job market.

She might very well say, ''Listen, Rick, I need some money to keep me going til I can get a job.'' Rick might say, ''Susan, why are you bothering me? I don't live with you anymore.'' Men are usually willing to support women as long as they live with them, but often not after they move out.

What can Susan do? If she were a legal wife, she could call a lawyer and he would take her case to domestic-relations court and obtain reasonable temporary support until a divorce settlement were reached or the case came up for trial. The court would probably order the husband to pay counsel fees so she could maintain the suit in domestic-relations court and be adequately represented. But because Susan is not a legal wife, but a cohabiting spouse, she must try for help in the civil court or court of common pleas on the grounds that a contractual agreement of some kind exists between her and Rick, or that there is some equitable basis for relief between the former partners.

Her first order of business, then, is to get a lawyer. She can look in the Yellow Pages of the telephone book for a lawyer who specializes in family law, because even though she probably cannot get into the domestic-relations side of the court, we are dealing with a family-law type of case. She can call the local bar association and ask for the names of lawyers who specialize in family law. The bar association will usually not recommend only one, but will give Susan the names of several lawyers to contact. Or she might have heard about a lawyer who has a reputation as a competent divorce specialist.

A woman who contacts a lawyer should normally be prepared to pay money by way of a retainer for that lawyer's services. If she cannot afford a lawyer she might contact the local legal-aid society, which will probably try to arrange for competent legal representation without initial remuneration. If she cannot get legal aid to handle the case, she might try one of the law ''clinics'' that are springing up throughout the country and offer adequate legal services at lower fees than their fellow practitioners.

The simple truth is that for a woman without funds, it is difficult to get a lawyer to handle a cohabitation case. She might be able to persuade a lawyer to handle her case on a contingency basis in states where that is acceptable. Divorce cases cannot normally be accepted on a contingency basis in some states—including California—but cohabitation cases can be at this early stage because there is no code of legislative restrictions that yet guides or limits fee arrangements with clients other than general ethical considerations preventing unconscionable charges.

Even if she has some money, it is difficult to get a lawyer to handle a cohabitation case because this is basically an uncharted field and the results are not uniform. It is still early in the game, euphemistically speaking. A young lawyer just starting out and without much business might be anxious to take such a case.

If the cohabiting spouse succeeds in obtaining a lawyer, he will first have to determine how the laws of that particular state apply. If it is in Phoenix, he might say, "Look, I'm sorry, but in Arizona it's a crime to cohabit. By statute, you cannot legally live with a man. It's a criminal act. There are no cases in Arizona that provide relief for women who live with men."

The woman might reply, "How would you like to be the first lawyer in Arizona to bring a case to challenge that law as was done in California?"

If they are in a state that has adopted the Marvin principles—in whole or in part, such as New Jersey, for example—the lawyer would probably try to determine if there was a written contract, or, if not, if there was an oral or implied agreement, and, if not, and he still believed the circumstances of the case were favorable enough, he could proceed with the object of recovering under some equitable remedy.

In such a case, a lawyer normally would first attempt to obtain some kind of temporary interim support for her. It would be routine for a legally married wife, but it will be difficult to obtain, temporarily at least, support outside of a family law court. In several cases I know of, however, it has been done.

Recently in San Diego Superior Court, a Lesbian was awarded temporary support. And even more recently, a former associate of mine, Donald Woldman, who worked on the original Marvin case, obtained a temporary-support order for his client in the Los Angeles Superior Court.

Unable to go into family-law court to seek temporary support for his client because there was no marriage and thus no standing in matrimonial law, Woldman applied civil law to bring about swift action in Los Angeles Superior Court. The fastest method of proceeding in civil court is by way of a show cause order and a temporary restraining order. This is a legal procedure to bring another party into court promptly—within a matter of days—and a way of freezing things as they are until the matter can be brought before a judge. Usually, the procedure is used to prevent another party from doing something that is detrimental to the moving party. Often, for instance, a party will obtain an order directing another party to show cause why he should not be prevented from disposing of business assets in which other parties have an interest.

Woldman obtained an order directing the defendant (male) to show cause why he should not be prevented from halting support to Woldman's woman client. He also obtained a temporary restraining order directing the defendant not to halt support and not to attempt to sell the house in which his client was residing.

In other words, by freezing things as they were through the use of a show cause order and a temporary restraining order, Woldman succeeded in maintaining conditions equal to an estranged wife's being provided with temporary support and shelter.

He had good authority for the action. In his memorandum of points and authorities, attached to the end of this chapter, he quotes former Presiding Judge Christian Markey of the Family Law Department of the Los Angeles Superior Court.

Of course, there should be favorable conditions for such a procedure to be effective. The woman should have been receiving support and must be in possession of the property in question. A show cause order and a temporary restraining order will only maintain the status quo; they will not bring about support payments when there were none before. There must be a showing that the party seeking help will be irrevocably harmed if the order is not granted.

Still, the effective application of the procedure is an important precedent. It is another avenue that may lead many unmarried cohabitants into court in timely fashion.

If temporary support cannot be obtained in a contract dispute, the client may wait a long time—perhaps three or four years—for his or her case to be heard on its merits.

If the case were admitted to the domestic-relations or family-law court, the litigation could probably get to trial within a year

—because the divorce calendar is normally designed to move faster than civil case matters.

The difference simply is that the wife usually receives needed support while awaiting trial and the disadvantaged cohabitant is left to shift on her own. This unfair treatment of women who find themselves in virtually the same position as wives when their mates walk out the front door or send them packing can be remedied, and I predict will be remedied, by prompt legislative enactment of the statutory law that allows unmarried cohabitants to process their grievances in the family-law courts where, I believe, these cases rightfully belong.

Another way to get quick action in a case dealing with an apparently solid written contract might be for the moving party's lawyer to make a motion for a summary judgment. A summary judgment is one entered by a judge without a trial where it can be shown that there is no arguable issue. If there are no disputed issues of fact, the motion may be granted and a final judgment quickly obtained. But it should be pointed out that if any kind of factual dispute is raised, such as fraud, undue influence or mistake, the case must be heard on its merits and the summary motion judgment will be denied.

Am I saying that fighting a cohabitation suit is very difficult and time-consuming? Yes, exactly. If you can settle such a dispute between yourselves, with lawyers to advise you, of course, you are well advised to do so. You not only save additional attorneys' fees and court costs, you save the anguish of a long, dry waiting spell and an uncertain result unless you have good evidence. Most cases that proceed through this difficult legal thicket are driven by a long and expensive investment and a continuing, desperate need for ultimate justice. On the other hand, am I saying that because of the time and expense involved—to say nothing of the acrimony that is certain to accompany the long battle —it is better to throw in the towel? The answer is an equally loud and clear, ''No!''

If it is a matter of conscience and real property rights are involved, then the quest for justice should be pursued and each individual should stand up and be counted. It then becomes a matter of personal ethics and morality.

A live-in contemplating such an action must also keep in mind that a statute of limitations controls such cases. Normally an oral contract has a two-year limitation period, after which time you can no longer bring a valid claim. In other words, a suit for breach of contract must be filed within a designated time period after the breakup.

The legal definition of the length of the statute of limitations can be difficult for the layman to understand and should be left to the lawyer to determine. Lawyers have tried to argue that in a three-year live-together relationship, the statute of limitations had run two years after the couple first hooked up. They are wrong—it does not work that way. But a cohabitant is advised not to wait until the last minute, remembering that once the case is filed, the time frame for getting to trial commences.

What live-togethers have to realize is that until the law catches up with this new class of people, it is going to be difficult and fluid and ever changing, growing and evolving as law always does. I originally predicted that within five years after the supreme court decision in the Marvin case every state would have either passed legislation or developed case law in the field. As of now, twenty-four states have adopted one or more of the Marvin principles as set forth in the original supreme court decision. Although not quite on schedule, we're almost halfway there, and enough progress has been made for me to conclude that the ship will eventually come into every court of call. We are again in the vanguard of the civil rights movement. That didn't happen overnight. It was a tortuous struggle. The development of the law in this field will also move slowly from the back of the bus to the front. But make no mistake, its time is near.

The Marvin principles as enumerated in the California Supreme Court decision will be codified and enacted into law by the various state legislatures. In other states, case law will develop. New Jersey adopted it completely in *Kozlowski* v. *Kozlowski*, and New York's highest court, in the case of *Morone* v. *Morone*, recently declared that oral contracts between cohabiting couples could be enforced.

Yes, there will be setbacks. In Illinois, after the court of appeals of that state applied the Marvin principles in the case of

Hewitt v. *Hewitt*, the Illinois Supreme Court reversed the appellate court on the basis of so-called "public policy" and denied all relief to Victoria Hewitt, who had lived with Dr. Robert M. Hewitt for fifteen years, borne him three children and helped him through dental school. By virtue of this misguided decision, the Illinois Supreme Court took one small step forward for man, but one giant step backward for both mankind and womankind in their quest for equal dignity and justice under the law.

Undoubtedly the Marvin decision, either by case law or statute, will be interpreted by state supreme courts and eventually by the United States Supreme Court.

Lawyers will be asked to take up the cudgels in such cases, to make new law in other states as *Marvin* v. *Marvin* did in California. It is a pioneering effort, a continuing struggle to redefine the rights of this new class, to give them new rights and to make them meaningful.

Cases will develop to win unmarried spouses the rights of interim temporary support, attorneys' fees *pedente lite*—pending litigation—so the deserted spouse can afford to bring an action, restraining orders to prevent the other spouse from disposing of property: all the rights enjoyed by married spouses.

We lawyers should be able to proceed in the cohabitation cases so that these disadvantaged people can obtain the equal protection of basic rights that licensed spouses now enjoy.

Temporary interim support should be predicated upon a typical divorce case. The plaintiff should receive temporary support upon a showing that she or he is unable to reasonably support herself, upon a showing of the wage-earning spouse's ability to provide support, and a showing of need and the life-style they previously enjoyed.

Simply stated, cohabitation cases must and will be processed through the family, matrimonial and domestic side of the court. Legislation is being pushed in many states to make cohabitation cases part of the family-law division. That is where they belong.

Here is attorney Donald Woldman's petition for a show cause order and a temporary restraining order, and his supporting memorandum of law.

The petition urges the court to direct the defendant (male) not to harass the plaintiff (female), not to try to sell off his property, not to halt support and to return the car she was using. The memorandum offers his legal arguments.

Los Angeles Superior Court Judge Vernon Foster granted his requests.

SUPERIOR COURT OF THE STATE OF CALIFORNIA FOR THE COUNTY OF LOS ANGELES

SARAH S., 　　　　　Plaintiff, 　　vs. WILLIAM T., et al., 　　　　　Defendants.	Case No. Order To Show Cause Re: Preliminary Injunction and Temporary Restraining Order

On reading the verified Complaint of Plaintiff on file in the above entitled action and the Declarations of Plaintiff and of DONALD WOLDMAN, and the Memorandum of Points and Authorities submitted herewith, and it appearing to the satisfaction of the Court that this is a proper cause for granting an Order to Show Cause and a Temporary Restraining Order, and that unless the Temporary Restraining Order prayed for be granted, great or irreparable injury will result to Plaintiff before the matter can be heard, on notice.

It is HEREBY ORDERED that the above named Defendant appear in Department 86 of this Court located at 111 North Hill Street, Los Angeles, California, on _____ at 9:00 A.M., or as soon thereafter as the matter may be heard, then and there to show cause, if any he has, why he and his agents, servants, employees, representatives and all persons acting in concert with him, should not be enjoined and restrained during the pendency of this action from engaging in, committing, or performing, directly or indirectly, any and all of the following acts:

1. Annoying, molesting or harassing Plaintiff in any manner whatsoever;

2. Selling, hypothecating or disposing of any of the following properties, other than in the ordinary course of business or necessities of life:

    (a) Residence at _____ ;
    (b) Real property at _____ ;
    (c) Apartment building located in _____ ;
    (d) Apartment building located in _____ ;
    (e) Apartment building located in _____ ;
    (f) Improved real property located in _____ .

3. Removing any items of furniture, furnishings or personal effects from the residence located in _____ .

IT IS FURTHER ORDERED that the above named Defendant shall appear at the same time and place and show cause, if any he has, why he should not be commanded by Order of this Court and required during the pendency of this action:

4. Not to interfere with Plaintiff's exclusive occupancy and control of the residence located in _____, and Defendant, his agents and/or representatives are ordered not to interfere or affect, directly or indirectly, Plaintiff's possession of said premises;

5. Continue to make all monthly trust deed payments related to the residence located in _____, and pay each and all real estate taxes as and when due;

6. Call Pacific Telephone and Telegraph Company to refer telephone calls for Plaintiff from her former telephone number to her new telephone number;

7. Keep in full force and effect all existing health and medical insurance for the benefit of Plaintiff;

8. Continue to pay for medical expenses of Plaintiff.

9. Continue to pay Plaintiff living expenses in a sum not to exceed $1,000.00 per month upon presentation to counsel for Defendant of bills therefor.

10. Continue to pay tuition, books, school supplies and related expenses for Plaintiff's medical school education upon presentation to counsel for Defendant of bills therefor;

11. Return to Plaintiff of her automobile for her continued exclusive use, possession and control.

IT IS FURTHER ORDERED that pending the hearing and determination of the Order to Show Cause, the above named Defendant, his officers, agents, employees, representatives and all persons acting in concert or participating with them, shall be and they are hereby restrained and enjoined from engaging in or performing, directly or indirectly, any and all of the following acts:

(Paragraphs 1. through 11 are repeated.)

IT IS FURTHER ORDERED that copies of the Declaration of Plaintiff, Memorandum of Points and Authorities and this Order to Show Cause and Temporary Restraining Order be served on Defendant not later than _____.

LET THE ABOVE ORDER ISSUE:

DATED: _____

_____

JUDGE OF THE SUPERIOR COURT

SUPERIOR COURT OF THE
STATE OF CALIFORNIA
FOR THE COUNTY OF LOS ANGELES

SARAH S.,
            Plaintiff,
 	
        vs.
 	
WILLIAM T., et al.,
            Defendants.
	Case No.
	
	Memorandum of Points and
	Authorities

As is set forth in the accompanying declarations and application for injunctive relief, this is a classic example of temporary support being awarded pendente lite.

In the new publication *California Family Law Practice and Procedure,* Markey, Vol. I—Cohabitation, Section 1.51, the former Presiding Judge of the Family Law Department of the Los Angeles Superior Court sets forth the applicable law applying directly to the facts presented in the case at Bar:

> "A nonmarital partner may be able to seek pendente lite support during the pendency of an action against the other partner to enforce property rights by means of an application for a preliminary injunction.

(See *Code of Civil Procedure* §527)

> "If the Defendant supported the Plaintiff during the time when the parties lived together, and if the Plaintiff has no other means of support, it would appear that a preliminary injunction would be available to prevent the Defendant from terminating support to the Plaintiff during the pendency of the litigation. This use of the preliminary injunction would be in keeping with the general rule that a preliminary injunction does not determine the ultimate rights of the parties, but preserves the status quo until a final determination of the merits of the action.

(Citing *Continental Banking Co.* v. *Katz* [1968] 68 Cal.2d 512)

> "Under the general heading of continuing the status quo pending determination of the merits of the action, a party may be ordered, by preliminary injunction, to continue regular and usual procedures.

(Citing *Fretz* v. *Burke* [1967] 247 Cal. App. 2d 741, 746)

> "A preliminary injunction may issue in an action at law, such as an action for damages, as well as in an equitable action, if it is reasonably necessary and fair to both sides to maintain the status quo pending the outcome of the litigation.

Lenard v. *Edmonds* [1957] 151 Cal.App.2d 764, 769)

> "Thus, pendente lite support by means of a permanent injunction appears potentially available regardless of the character of relief sought by the Plaintiff nonmarital partner in the underlying action."

In the case at Bar, there can be no doubt that these are the classic circumstances discussed by Judge Markey in his publication. Plaintiff has been in a position of dependency as a result of her muscular dystrophy disease and of her continued need and necessity for receiving support for payment of her medical expenses, living expenses and educational expenses.

It is therefore requested that this Court in equity and good conscience not allow Plaintiff to be placed into a position of being put on welfare as a result of her prior years' reliance upon Defendant for support.

The Court's attention is drawn to the showing, vis-à-vis the canceled checks and other supporting documentation, concerning both the nature of investments made by Plaintiff of funds which she then had and her receipt of support from Defendant.

RESPECTFULLY SUBMITTED:

DONALD N. WOLDMAN
A Professional Corporation

By _____
DONALD N. WOLDMAN
Attorney for Plaintiff

6

"ODD COUPLE"

RELATIONSHIPS

TRYING TO ESTIMATE the number of homosexuals in the nation is even more difficult than trying to count the unmarried couples. In fact, from my experience, I have found that it is impossible. Gay groups I questioned would not even risk an estimate. We know only that the number is considerable, that there appear to be gay communities in every city, that gays are in every profession from show business to fashion and from the National Football League to the U.S. armed forces. It is not the purpose of this book to perform such a census. Their numbers, we may safely conclude, are extensive and probably in the millions.

History records homosexuals from ancient times. *Lesbian* comes from *Lesbos*, the ancient Greek isle that was traditionally the home of "female homosexuals." The eleventh letter of the Greek alphabet, Lambda, is considered the traditional symbol of homosexuality. Ancient writings abound with references to gay men. The greatest Roman of them all, Julius Caesar, was considered gay or bisexual by some of his contemporaries. The gossipy Roman historian Suetonius tells us that as a young man Caesar had a homosexual liaison with King Nicomedes of Bithynia. Caesar's sexual appetite did not exclude women, of course. His female paramours included many of the noblest ladies of Rome—not to mention Queen Cleopatra of Egypt. Because of his bisexual activities, the orator Curio the Elder made a remark famous among Roman contemporaries that Caesar was "every woman's man and every man's woman." It is not my purpose to trace homosexual history; I note only that references to homosexuals go back to Sodom and before.

In the eyes of the law, gay relationships fall into the same category as the meretricious spouse. They are beyond the boundaries of the court of domestic relations and must take their cases into the civil court or court of common pleas as contract matters. Although many gay couples consider themselves as married as it is humanly possible to be, such unions have no real legal recognition in the United States. As far as I have been able to determine, there is no legal recognition of a same-sex marriage anywhere in the Western world. Some gays are under the impression that Holland or Denmark has legalized gay marriage or common-law gay marriage, but they are mistaken and apparently are referring to the social acceptance of a sort of unmarried cohabitation in those countries. Unmarried cohabitation by couples of any combination is becoming socially acceptable abroad, as it is here, but there is as yet no legal recognition of marriage for same-sex couples. "Decriminalizing" same-sex relationships does not constitute granting these couples the legal status of husband and wife. And not all states in the United States have decriminalized homosexual relationships, either, as we shall see.)

Gay couples are able to be united in religious marriage ceremonies, however. The Metropolitan Community Church, a national denomination of gay churches, performs same-sex marriages. Some Unitarian and Universalist churches also perform them, at the discretion of the individual ministers. Various other groups also perform ceremonies or weddings.

These religious celebrations do not have the force of lawful marriages, however, and they are not legally recognized despite their churchly sanction. They will not open the doors of the court of domestic relations or of probate court for homosexual couples. These rites are ceremonial only. Under the law, a wedding and a marriage are not the same thing.

There have been several attempts by gay couples to have legal marriages performed or to have marriages that already have been performed recognized by law.

These same-sex couples have been confronted by the established public policy that marriage is fundamentally the union of one man and one woman for the purpose of procreating children.

In 1971, Richard John Baker and James Michael McConnell went to Gerald Nelson, clerk of Hennepin County in Minneapolis, Minnesota, and applied for a marriage license. Nelson refused to issue such a license. Baker, who carried the case forward, brought a writ of mandamus proceeding, which sought to order Nelson to issue such a license. But the district court judge quashed the writ and specifically directed Nelson *not* to issue a license. Baker then appealed to the Minnesota Supreme Court.

In his petition on behalf of Baker, attorney R. Michael Wetherbee argued that because there was no state statute on the books in Minnesota against same-sex marriage, it was the intent of the legislature to authorize such marriages.

He also contended that denial of same-sex marriages violated the First, Eighth, Ninth and Fourteenth Amendments to the United States Constitution.

In his opinion for the Minnesota Supreme Court, Associate Justice C. Donald Peterson declared that state law could not be construed as authorizing same-sex marriage. "We think . . . that a sensible reading of the statute discloses a contrary intent," he wrote.

The opinion stated that the statute employed the term "marriage" in the common usage to mean a union between persons of the opposite sex. It offered *Webster's New International Dictionary,* third edition, definition: "1a: the state of being united to a person of the opposite sex as husband or wife," and also the definition from *Black's Law Dictionary:* "Marriage . . . is the civil status, condition, or relation of one man and one woman united in law for life, for the discharge to each other and the community of the duties legally incumbent on those whose association is founded on the distinction of sex.''

''It is unrealistic to think that the original draftsmen of our marriage statutes, which date from territorial days, would have used the term in any different sense,'' the court said. ''The term is of contemporary significance as well, for the present status is replete with words of heterosexual import such as 'husband and wife' and 'bride and groom.'

''We hold therefore that Minnesota (law) does not authorize marriage between persons of the same sex and that such marriages are accordingly prohibited.''

Having held that Minnesota does not and never has authorized same-sex marriages but, on the contrary, prohibits them, the court considered the matter of whether such a holding violates the U.S. Constitution.

Baker v. *Nelson* argued that forbidding Baker and McConnell to marry denied fundamental rights, including those guaranteed under the First, Eighth, Ninth and Fourteenth Amendments. The courts dismissed without comment the contention that the denial of same-sex marriage offended the First and Eighth Amendments. The First Amendment protects the rights of religion, of freedom of speech and of the press, of peaceable assembly and of the right to petition for redress of grievances. Whether the argument was that homosexual religious groups authorized gay marriages and that the law cannot therefore deny them, or that the case amounted to a petition to redress a grievance isn't known, because the court declined to consider that point. As to the Eighth Amendment, which prohibits ''cruel and unusual punishment,'' the court again dismissed the argument without discussion.

It did, however, address itself to the contention that the denial offended the Ninth and Fourteenth Amendments. The Ninth declares: ''The enumeration in the Constitution, of certain rights, shall not be construed to deny or disparage others retained by the people.''

In other words, any rights not expressly denied are retained by the people.

The Fourteenth Amendment, adopted in 1868 to protect the

rights of former slaves, states in part that citizens may not be deprived of life, liberty or property "without due process of law," nor may they be denied the "equal protection of the law." It also states that "no state shall make or enforce any law which shall abridge the privileges or immunities of citizens of the United States."

And so *Baker* v. *Nelson* was contending that there was no law on the Minnesota books prohibiting marriage and that the U.S. Constitution said that any rights not expressly denied are retained by the people. It also argued that, because citizens must not be denied "equal protection of the law," Baker and McConnell were not being treated the same as, say, Robert Smith and Mary Jones.

Justice Peterson responded: "These constitutional challenges have in common the assertion that the right to marry without regard to the sex of the parties is a fundamental right of all persons and that restricting marriage to only couples of the opposite sex is irrational and invidiously discriminatory. We are not independently persuaded by these contentions and do not find support for them in any decisions of the United States Supreme Court."

Then, redefining marriage in legal terms, the court said: "The institution of marriage as a union of a man and a woman, uniquely involving the procreation and rearing of children within a family, is as old as the book of Genesis. This historic institution manifestly is more deeply founded than the asserted contemporary concept of marriage and societal interests for which petitioners contend. The due process clause of the Fourteenth Amendment is not a charter for restructuring it by judicial legislation.

"The equal protection clause of the Fourteenth Amendment, like the due process clause, is not offended by the state's classification of persons authorized to marry," the opinion went on. "There is no irrational or invidious discrimination.

"Petitioners note that the state does not impose upon heterosexual married couples a condition that they have a proved capacity or declared willingness to procreate, posing a rhetorical demand that this court must read such conditions into the statute if same-sex marriages are to be prohibited. Even assuming that such a condition would be neither unrealistic nor offensive . . . the classification is no more than theoretically imperfect."

The court then quoted an earlier ruling: "The Constitution does not require things which are different in fact or opinion to be treated in law as though they were the same."

In conclusion, the Minnesota Supreme Court opinion said: "We hold, therefore, that [the Minnesota state statute prohibiting marriage] does not offend the First, Eighth, Ninth or Fourteenth Amendments to the United States Constitution. Affirmed."

Thus, the Minnesota State Supreme Court held that same-sex marriages may not be legally performed. *Baker* v. *Nelson* remains the prevailing case law in the field.

A similar case, this one involving two women, occurred in Kentucky in 1973 and was eventually decided by the Kentucky Court of Appeals. In that case, *Jones* v. *Hallahan,* a county clerk refused to issue a marriage license to two females. The women plaintiffs offered several of the same arguments put forth in *Baker* v. *Nelson,* to wit: that denying them a marriage license deprived them of their constitutional rights to marry, of association, free exercise of religion, and that it subjected them to cruel and unusual punishment. They also argued that there was no Kentucky statute prohibiting same-sex marriage.

The Kentucky Court of Appeals noted that although state law did not define marriage, "common dictionary definitions of the term clearly define the relationship as a legal union between one man and one woman." It added: "Two women are prevented from marrying, not by state law or by the refusal of a local official to issue a marriage license to them, but by their own incapacity of entering into a marriage as that term is defined.

"A license to enter into a status or a relationship which the parties are incapable of achieving is a nullity," the court declared. "If the (two women) had concealed from the clerk the fact that they were of the same sex and he had issued a license to them and a ceremony had been performed, the resulting relationship would not constitute a marriage."

The court pointed out that *Baker* v. *Nelson* had already "considered many of the constitutional issues raised by the appellants here and decided them adversely to (the two women). In our view, however, no constitutional issue is involved. We find no constitutional sanction or protection of the right of marriage between two persons of the same sex."

And *Jones* v. *Hallahan* is the prevailing case law concerning Lesbian marriages.

Not only have the courts refused to allow same-sex marriages of gay couples, they have also held that if such a marriage is performed, it is legally null and void.

The 1971 case of *Anonymous* v. *Anonymous* in the matrimonial part of Queens Supreme Court in New York City dealt with the issue. It involved a U.S. Army noncomissioned officer whom we'll call Sergeant Presten. Presten met a "woman" on the street in Augusta, Georgia, in November of 1968. He and the woman —a hooker, she said—went to a house of prostitution where they had some laughs together; but he did not see the hooker undressed nor did they have sexual relations.

In February of 1969, Presten reported to his new assignment at Fort Hood, Texas, and the hooker turned into a camp follower, trailing him to his new base. On February 22, 1969, Presten and his friend were united by a marriage ceremony in Belton, Texas, and returned to the sergeant's apartment. The sergeant was drunk and fell asleep, as he declared later in court papers.

When Presten awakened at two o'clock in the morning and reached for his "bride," he "discovered that the [bride] had male sexual organs," according to the court papers.

"He immediately left the bed, 'got drunk some more,' and went to the bus station," apparently intending to put as much distance as he could between himself and his new "wife."

But the sergeant found no bus that night and eventually returned home to sleep on the sofa. His "bride" told the sergeant that he intended to undergo an operation to have the male sex organs removed.

Sergeant Presten went overseas in March of 1969 and returned in April of 1970, having received letters and medical bills for hospital and surgical expenses from his "wife." The Army also deducted an allotment from Presten's pay for the spouse.

Upon his return to the States, Presten met his spouse in San Francisco, and they traveled together to New York City—the sergeant's home. On the trip, the spouse told Sergeant Presten that the sex surgery had been completed and that the spouse was now a woman.

Sergeant Presten, however, filed his suit in Queens Supreme Court seeking a legal declaration of his marital status. His spouse hired a lawyer to contest the action, and then left once more for the West Coast, never to be heard from again, except to send Sergeant Presten bills for charged merchandise.

Supreme Court Justice Albert Buschmann heard the case in the matrimonial part of Queens Supreme Court, which is the court of domestic relations, and declared: "The court finds as a fact that the defendant was not a female at the time of the marriage ceremony. It may be that since that time the defendant's sex has been changed to female by operative procedures, although it would appear from the medical articles and other information supplied by counsel that mere removal of the male organs would not, in and of itself, change a person into a true female.

"The law makes no provision for a 'marriage' between persons of the same sex. Marriage is and always has been a contract between a man and a woman," he said.

As in the other two cases, the judge offered definitions of legal marriage: "*Black's Law Dictionary* furnishes three definitions of marriage, all of which recognize that it is a union or contract between a man and a woman."

He cited a case in point—*Mirizio* v. *Mirizio:* "The mere fact that the law provides that physical incapacity for sexual relationship shall be ground for annulling a marriage is of itself sufficient indication of the public policy that such relationship shall exist with the result and for the purpose of begetting offspring."

Justice Buschmann then reasoned that in *Anonymous* v. *Anonymous* there were not even grounds for annulling Sergeant Presten's marriage because no marriage could have ever existed. There are "two basic requirements for a marriage contract, i.e., a man and a woman. Here, one of these basic requirements was missing.

"The marriage ceremony itself was a nullity. No legal relationship could be created by it," he said. "Accordingly, the court declares that the so-called marriage ceremony in which the plaintiff and defendant took part in Belton, Texas, on February 22, 1969, did not in fact or in law create a marriage contract and that the plaintiff and defendant are not and have not ever been 'husband and wife' or parties to a valid marriage.''

These three decisions, all recent and cases of first impression (that is, without precedent) in each state, establish case law that makes same-sex marriage illegal—at least in these states—whether by two men, two women or in a case in which one of the parties is unaware that he is entering into a same-sex marriage.

The same problem arises when a same-sex spouse attempts to inherit property on the grounds that a family type of relationship existed. In 1979, Stanley Saul went into New York City Housing Court and sought to claim title to a Manhattan cooperative apartment that was owned by his partner of ten years, writer Philip J. Perl, of *The New Yorker* magazine, who had died.

Saul argued that he and Perl "for all intents and purposes lived as a family unit," and that a family is not restricted to "relatives by blood or marriage."

The two men "lived together for ten years, shared the same household and its expenses, ate at the same table and slept in the same bedroom, wore each other's clothes, enjoyed the same friends, attended the same social functions, took vacations together and operated for all purposes as a family," Saul argued in court papers.

It was a clear case of arguing that although a legal marriage did not exist, there was cohabitation that amounted to a de facto marriage.

But Judge Ferdinand Pellegrino, after researching the case, held that: "The court has been unable to find any authority that holds that homosexuals living together constitute a family unit."

The judge noted that Perl had owned the apartment solely in his own name for fifteen years, that "no marriage ceremony was ever performed between them," and that when Perl bought the cooperative apartment he had not listed Saul as a relative. The apartment in the Penn South cooperative reverted to Perl's estate and then back to the co-op.

It should be noted here that if Perl had put Saul's name on the title deed as coowner, there might have been no problem. He could also have left the property to Saul in his will, although even that legal device has been challenged successfully in the case of homosexuals.

There was a case, *In re Kaufman's Will,* in which a homosexual legally left property to his lover. But the dead man's heirs went to court to upset the will on the grounds that the man was under "undue influence" and "not of sound mind" when he made the bequest. The will was declared null and void, and the property went to the deceased's partner's heirs.

Such are the problems of homosexuals in attempting to establish ties of family or marriage.

There was one example of homosexuals marrying legally, however. In Boulder, Colorado, after an ordinance was passed prohibiting discrimination against homosexuals, six gay couples presented themselves before the city clerk and demanded to be married. The clerk, apparently not knowing what to do, married them. Presumably these couples will be legally married as long as no one challenges their unions. Probably, however, the marriages could not withstand any kind of a legal attack, and these people would be well advised to consider their marriages ceremonial only.

Not only does prevailing case law hold that homosexual couples cannot legally marry, but there is the additional bar in most states that sexual acts between same-sex couples are a crime, just as cohabitation between unmarried members of the opposite sex is a crime in nineteen states.

Attempts by the gay world to overturn state laws that prohibit homosexual acts between consenting adults have not, to date, demonstrably succeeded either. In 1976, an anti-sodomy law in Virginia was upheld by the U.S. Supreme Court without comment. Again in 1979, the U.S. Supreme Court let stand the conviction of a North Carolina man for sodomy. In that case, Eugene Enslin of Jacksonville was convicted in 1974 under the North Carolina state statute of "an abominable and detestable crime against nature." The state law declares: "If any person shall commit the crime against nature, with mankind or beast, he shall be guilty of a felony and shall be fined or imprisoned in the discretion of the court." Enslin, who was convicted in a case involving a young U.S. Marine from Camp LeJeune, North Carolina, was sentenced to a year in prison.

The thrust of these High Court rulings is that the individual states' right to enact laws governing homosexual acts shall not be questioned by the U.S. Supreme Court. This double impediment, first, that homosexuals may not legally marry or establish familial ties through de facto or common-law marriages and, second, that homosexual acts are criminal in most states (which means gay marriages are not only not recognized but criminal), creates a significant and seemingly insurmountable barrier to legal gay marriage. It suggests that, as with heterosexual unmarried couples, a living-together agreement is the only alternative and can be the only true "marriage."

A ceremonial "wedding" plus a legal, written contract appears within the reach of all gay couples. Homosexual live-together agreements are, in effect, ordinary business contracts. Just as a straight couple's agreement contains no mention of sexual relations, a gay or Lesbian agreement also has no such references. Any suggestion that the business contract involved sex would, of course, make it illegal and unenforceable. Instead, it sets forth the parties' ownership of property and how it shall be disposed of in case the "business" is ended. Agreements that are not sufficiently businesslike may not stand up in court.

Judges have been known to "look behind the agreement" and find that it was based upon a homosexual relationship and, therefore, not valid. If, for example, only one of the partners owns any property and also contributes all the earnings, the other party may have great difficulty recovering half of the property in case the wage earner should die. Even if the property-owning partner has left a will bequeathing the property to his or her partner, the agreement might be successfully challenged if other heirs exist who have been ignored. Homosexual wills, in other words, must be written very carefully. A "divorce" proceeding in such a case would be heard in the civil court or court of common pleas, just as it is for any other couple who are not legally married.

Although gay couples have not as yet—and may never—achieve legal status as married couples, there has been some success in gaining custody of children, either their own in divorce situations, or through adoption.

In a Minneapolis case, Judge Robert Bowen of Hennepin County Family Court granted a Lesbian mother permanent custody of her three children, boys aged four, ten and twelve, ruling that her homosexuality did not prevent her from being a proper mother. The husband, Jerry, had challenged a temporary-custody arrangement that allowed his wife, Carol, to keep the children. The husband argued that the mother's lesbianism could influence his sons to become homosexual. The judge disagreed, saying that both Jerry and Carol were "good parents," and allowed her to retain custody.

A rather remarkable case occurred in 1979 in Greene County Family Court in Catskill, New York, concerning a thirteen-year-old boy named Alden who had been adopted by minister Johannes Kuiper, thirty-six, of the Reformed Church of America. Alden had been living with Reverend Kuiper, a naturalized citizen from Holland, for a year when the minister came out publicly and announced that he had a homosexual lover. Judge James Battista then decided to review the adoption, and Kuiper's church started proceedings to cancel Kuiper's ordination.

After reexamining the case of young Alden, Judge Battista granted Reverend Kuiper permanent custody of the boy. "The reverend is providing a good home; the boy loves his adoptive father, and wants to be with him," Judge Battista declared. "The man doesn't beat his son, and when you look at all the cases of child abuse you get from so-called 'straights,' you gasp for words."

Kuiper took a job as a waiter in nearby Albany and assumed new duties in Albany as pastor of the Good News Metropolitan Community Church, which deals mostly with the gay community.

Kuiper previously had been married for eight years and said he didn't realize he was gay until he was thirty-six. He said he didn't think his own homosexuality would influence his son.

"I'm sure he's straight, and that's fine with me," said Kuiper. "I'm not setting up any goals for him because we homosexuals are very sensitive to civil rights, to letting people do what they want. To tell you the truth, I'm glad he's the way he is for two reasons; one, because it will make it easier for him, and two, because I want grandchildren."

And so that appears to be a situation in which a gay man did achieve a family relationship, and may become a grandparent, too.

The fact that gay couples cannot be legally married—though they can be married in a religious ceremony—does not save them from the usual stresses of married or cohabiting couples, of course. They have the identical problems—from who should wash the dishes to sexual fidelity—that concern heterosexual couples. They even go to "marriage counselors"—who are called "couple counselors."

At one such facility, the Homosexual Community Counseling Center in New York City, gays sounded off like any married people. "I don't like doing all the housework," said a Lesbian. "I am not capable of being faithful to one person forever and ever," said a gay male.

Dr. Charles Silverstein, a psychologist who specializes in the treatment of homosexuals, insists the stereotypes about homosexuals—that they are basically miserable and that their relationships are unstable—are simply not true. "We met many gay couples here in New York City who've been together twenty, thirty or forty years," he said in a *New York Times* interview. "They aren't dancing at Studio 54 or fooling around in gay bars. They're living quiet lives that no one sees. This is not just in the cities but absolutely everywhere. I've been down in the Bible Belt and seen, in the same town with fundamentalist churches, gay lovers in very stable relationships. No one bothers them."

Gay couples attending a conference sponsored by the Homosexual Community Counseling Center sounded like middle-class heterosexual couples discussing their problems.

Said a thirty-year-old salesman named Lewis, "I was getting confused between the physical commitment and what I really felt toward Vince, aside from sex. It took me a year to work this out on my own and another year for us to work this out together."

Susan, who works in magazine publishing, talked about her Lesbian relationship with Bobby, a researcher in child welfare: "Bobby washes the dishes and cooks, not because I force it on her, but because it is her preference." Bobby added, "In heterosexual marriages, the husband is expected to mow the grass on Saturday. We both hate to mow the grass to we decided to hire somebody to do it." "And we have a cleaning woman who comes in once a week," said Susan.

There are also the problems of sexual infidelity, which are just as difficult as with straight couples, but apparently not more so.

Couple counselors also help gay couples talk about written contracts between them to protect themselves in the event of a breakup. Denied the security of such protection that flows from a legal marriage, a contract agreement is the only protection available to gay couples.

More and more gay couples are buying property together, including houses in the suburbs. With the passage of anti-discrimination laws—which were designed to help women or single people but also help gays indirectly—gays are able to obtain mortgage loans.

Homosexuals who buy homes in the suburbs are frequently fleeing an unhappy life in the city or seeking privacy. They are more often the type who are not activists and either do not wish to advertise their homosexuality or might be concealing it.

"We certainly don't tell the agents we are gay when we go looking for a house," one commented.

There is also the problem of discrimination from suburban neighbors if they find out a new couple is a homosexual household instead of two straight singles living together. There may be more tolerance in the anonymity of a large city than on a suburban street, where neighbors may react quite differently. One gay man who tried to buy a house in an elegant suburb discovered this to his anguish.

"I was offering her full price—$100,000 in cash," he said. "It was when I told her I was gay that she refused to sell, saying she couldn't do such a thing to her neighbors. They didn't want their children influenced by a homosexual. She became hysterical. And then she turned right around and sold the house to somebody for only $85,000."

Connecticut State Senator Betty Hudson, who has pushed for many anti-discrimination bills in the fields of jobs and housing, noted: "The families are terrified for their children. Parents are afraid that children will be molested or that these people will also become role models for their sons and daughters. That is where the trouble really lies."

For those reasons, and because suburban gays are often still "in the closet," home buying is cautious and the houses sought are those in secluded settings surrounded by trees.

"They will never go for a home on a family-type block if they can avoid it," a real estate agent said. "They much prefer the 'hidden house' in the trees. I think they overcome a lot of potential trouble this way."

In such relationships, where the gay couple prefers that the neighbors do not know they are gay, there is often a "strong" and a "weak" partner. Often the strong partner becomes the title holder of the property.

It can be easily seen that such situations could leave the weak partner in an unfortunate situation should the couple break up or if the strong partner dies first. That is why, at house closings involving gay couples, there is often a written contract arranged to protect both parties.

"Sometimes they will deed half an interest, or agree to cosign the note," a real estate agent said. "Occasionally an agreement is no more than a handshake. Litigation? It never ends up in court."

The real estate agent may think she understands gays as special people when she says that. I submit that she is incorrect about such cases never ending up in court. We have already cited such a case involving Saul and Perl and a Manhattan cooperative apartment.

At any rate, as has been stressed repeatedly, when property enters the picture, trouble may not be far behind. If two gays buy a house and only one has his or her name on the title, the other party is in the same situation as a meretricious spouse; in fact, he or she may be in a worse position, because the Marvin decision has not yet been extended to homosexuals.

Nevertheless, inroads have been made. As previously pointed out, a San Diego court awarded temporary support to a Lesbian partner while the principles awaited a full trial on the merits of the case. There are many legal experts who believe that although legal recognition of gay marriage will not be readily forthcoming, the protection of the legal umbrella will include gays' rights to proceed in cohabitation cases by way of contract and equitable remedies such as are currently being afforded straight couples.

The chilling public embarrassment attending palimony cases prevents many abandoned live-in women from taking their claims to court. There must be much at stake for such a case to reach trial. This natural reluctance to air dirty linen in public is greatly increased in gay cases. That's why many such cases carry the citation *Anonymous* v. *Anonymous*.

In addition to the public humiliation, judges and court personnel have been known to be unsympathetic or even hostile toward parties to litigation involving gays.

Roz Richter, executive director of the Lambda Legal Defense and Education Fund, Inc., at 132 West Forty-third Street, New York City, a group that fights for homosexual rights, commented: "There's been a long history of sexual hostility against minorities in the courts. It's not just in terms of what happens legally. You're asking Lesbians and gay men to go before a judge who has no grasp of their experience. It's so difficult that many gay and Lesbian couples just don't bother. And that can leave a pall over a breakup."

Richter described what she said was the "oppressive nature of the court system." It exists, she said, "on all sorts of connotative levels. There's a lack of sympathy and understanding."

In addition to the hostility felt by homosexuals, there is also the problem that civil courts and the court of common pleas are "slow and expensive, and lack flexibility," she said. All defendants, gay or straight, suffer from the deficiencies of the court system.

Richter recalled a case involving a gay couple who had lived together for fifteen years.

"They had bought a house together," she said. "They had put everything they had into it. Then, they broke up. One party really wanted to keep the house, and the other one didn't care that much. But the one who didn't care about the house needed his money out of it."

The partner who needed his money had to go to court and petition for a partition of the property to get his rightful half. "The only way to do it was to sell the house and split the proceeds," she said.

The case had nothing to do with the fact that the two men were gay. It was a business agreement that could have been between any two people—including a cohabitating couple or two straight singles. It could have been property owned by a business.

Because of dissatisfaction with the traditional court system, the Lambda Legal Defense and Education Fund has launched the Lambda Arbitration Project to study and draw up recommendations for an alternative, nonjudicial system of solving the problems of gay couples.

"We're planning to establish a way to avoid the adversarial process, as well as the hostility, slowness and inflexibility of the court system," said Richter.

According to Richter, the plan is to establish three-member panels to serve as arbitration panels, to which gay couples could voluntarily submit their problems for settlement. It would be, in effect, a voluntary, private court for homosexuals.

Some labor unions and some church groups settle their own disputes by arbitration without going through the courts, so the process has been used before and it is a workable and tested idea.

As envisioned, as many as fifty panels will be formed to handle homosexual "divorces." The Lambda Arbitration Project expects it will have to train the panelists.The project will have to rent space for its "courts," and the target date for putting the arbitration sessions into action is the end of 1980.

Gay couples are like any couples who live together without going through a formal marriage, said Richter. "Most typical couples live together and acquire property together," she continued. "They don't draw up agreements in advance for the same reason that heterosexual couples don't. Either they don't think of it, or it's too formal and cold."

Just as with a straight couple, the dissolution of a gay relationship involves a division of property. Such a couple might find what Richter calls a "less confrontational stance" in front of a Lambda Arbitration Project panel.

"That couple who had to sell the house and divide up the money—they might have been able to work out a payment plan and to have let one keep the house," she said. "We hope for more room for nontraditional ways to resolve such disputes."

The arbitration would be, as indicated, voluntary on the part of the couples who sought its help. Depending upon how much property was involved, either or both of the parties might be represented by legal counsel. The cost of the arbitration would be borne by the litigants.

"We're thinking of a sliding fee schedule," said the executive director. "Or, we might work out charges for progressive hearings. The first one would be free; the second would cost something, and the third would cost more. That system is standard in arbitration systems. We're seeking funding and hope to begin by the end of 1980. We need $5,000 or $10,000 to get it off the ground —for training manuals and to get things going."

The Lambda executive expects no financial problems, once the project is under way. "We expect that in the first year it will pay for itself," she said.

Through the arbitration device, gay parties to a property dispute will be able to work out a contract agreeable to both and to bargain out of the relationship. Once a contract has been reached to the satisfaction of both, it could be filed as an agreement that would have full legal force. It would have all the legal force of a divorce decree.

The panel will also be able to handle written agreements that gay couples work up in advance, for those who can handle them.

Through such bodies as the Lambda Arbitration Panel, an eminently practical idea that seems certain to spread to other homosexual communities across the nation, or through a combination of religious weddings and express written agreements, gay couples can find workable alternatives to legal marriage and divorce, and therefore achieve a status not unlike that of millions of other couples—even though that may not be entirely what they have in mind.

Here are two sample agreements for gays. Each of these could be drawn up in advance and if the parties eventually decided to terminate the relationship, the agreement could be submitted to the Lambda Arbitration Project or another self-help organization for arbitration.

In the first agreement, Smith and Jones both convey half of their current property to the other, and also provide that they will share equally all property that either may acquire in the future.

Either party may terminate the agreement—or get a "divorce" —by written notice to the other. The two parties to the agreement recognize that a "divorce" might involve difficulties in division of property, and so they stipulate that in case of a dispute the matter will be submitted to the Lambda Arbitration Project. Some agreements stipulate additional arbitrators in case the first one cannot or will not handle the dispute.

In the second agreement, between Johnson and Anderson, the agreement is only to cohabit in a house (or cooperative apartment) that the parties have purchased together. The agreement reflects that one party has put up two-thirds of the money and the other one-third, and that if the property is sold that shall be the division of value. Johnson and Anderson either have not heard of Lambda, or have decided to submit any dispute that may arise to civil court as a contract matter.

AGREEMENT OF ADAM SMITH AND TOM JONES

ADAM SMITH, hereinafter "SMITH," and TOM JONES, hereinafter "JONES," mutually agree as follows:

1. The purpose of this agreement is to make express the parties' agreement concerning the ownership and disposition of their property which they have in the past acquired and may in the future acquire.

2. "Property" as used herein shall mean all property both real and personal, regardless of the date, source, or manner of acquisition.

3. The agreement shall be governed by the law of the State of _____.

4. SMITH and JONES agree that SMITH's property currently held and JONES's property currently held are of approximately equal value. SMITH hereby conveys to JONES a fifty percent (50%) interest in all property which SMITH currently holds; and JONES hereby conveys to SMITH a fifty percent (50%) interest in all property which JONES currently holds; each in consideration of the conveyance of the other.

5. SMITH and JONES, recognizing that each party has the current ability to support himself and wishing to provide for the future well-being, security and support of the other, hereby mutually convey, each to the other, a fifty percent (50%) interest in all property which each shall in the future acquire. The parties expressly intend that this provision shall apply to all property rights including, but not limited to, pensions, disability income, unemployment compensation, options, and all interests both legal and equitable, whether or not such interest is vested.

6. All transfers of property including gifts by either SMITH or JONES shall be deemed a transfer by both parties, provided that each party has actual notice of the transfer prior to delivery of the property or gives written confirmation of the transfer after delivery of the property.

7. Policies of insurance on the life of either party in existence as of the date of this agreement shall not be covered by this agreement, provided, however, that any such policy shall not be modified to provide for benefits not provided by the terms of such policy as it exists as of the date of this agreement.

8. This agreement may be terminated by either party by serving upon the other party a written notice that the agreement is terminated.

9. Termination of this agreement will affect only property acquired after the date of termination. All property acquired prior to the date of written notice of termination shall be governed by this agreement.

10. If any provision of this agreement shall be held unenforceable such provision shall be deemed severed from the agreement and the remainder of the agreement shall be enforceable.

11. If upon termination of this agreement the parties are unable to agree between themselves upon a division of property, the matter shall be submitted to The Lambda Arbitration Project of New York City, New York, for arbitration. The decision of The Lambda Arbitration Project as to the division of the property shall be final and binding upon both of the parties.

12. Arbitration may be commenced by either party by submitting a copy of this agreement and a copy of written notice of termination as provided for in paragraph 8 above to The Lambda

Arbitration Project. The arbitrator shall give thirty (30) days written notice to each party of the date and time of hearing and shall otherwise have complete discretion in selecting the place, time and procedure for hearing.

13. The fee charged by the Lambda Arbitration Project for the settlement of the dispute shall be paid by the parties upon submission of the dispute for settlement, each party to pay one-half of said fee.

14. Should litigation be instituted to enforce any of the terms of this agreement, the prevailing party shall be entitled to recover a reasonable attorney's fee.

DATED: _____   _____
                                 (Signed) ADAM SMITH

DATED: _____   _____
                                 (Signed) TOM JONES

AGREEMENT OF JANE JOHNSON AND BARBARA ANDERSON

JANE JOHNSON (hereinafter "JOHNSON") and BARBARA ANDERSON (hereinafter "ANDERSON"), mutually agree as follows:

1. The purpose of this agreement is to make express the parties' agreement concerning the ownership and disposition of their property, including the real property commonly known as _____*(Address)*_____, and any and all other property which they have in the past acquired and may in the future acquire.

2. "Property" as used herein shall mean all property both real and personal, regardless of the date, source or manner of acquisition.

3. This agreement shall be governed by the law of the State of _____.

4. JOHNSON and ANDERSON state that it is their intention to cohabit at _____*(Address)*_____; JOHNSON and ANDERSON agree that their respective earnings are their sole

and separate property, regardless of whether they shall continue to cohabit at _____*(Address)*_____, or at any other location.

5. JOHNSON and ANDERSON mutually agree that there is no agreement between them, either express or implied, to provide support, maintenance, or in any other way share their earnings and accumulations.

6. Only that property which is expressly by written agreement held in joint tenancy or tenancy in common shall be deemed to be mutually held by the parties to this agreement.

7. JOHNSON and ANDERSON agree that the real property commonly known as _____*(Address)*_____ is held by the parties as a tenancy in common, pursuant to fiduciary deed dated _____. The parties agree that an undivided two-thirds (⅔) interest in said property is held by JOHNSON, and an undivided one-third (⅓) interest in said property is held by ANDERSON.

8. The parties agree that JOHNSON has paid two-thirds (⅔) of the down payment on the aforementioned real property, and ANDERSON has paid one-third (⅓) of the down payment on the aforementioned real property. The parties further agree that two-thirds (⅔) of the costs of all improvements and maintenance of said property, along with two-thirds (⅔) of all payments on the deed of trust on said real property, shall be paid by JOHNSON. ANDERSON shall pay one-third (⅓) of the costs of all improvements and maintenance for said real property along with one-third (⅓) of each payment due on said deed of trust on said property.

9. JOHNSON and ANDERSON agree that the proceeds from any sale of the aforementioned real property shall be divided two-thirds (⅔) to JOHNSON and one-third (⅓) to ANDERSON.

10. In the event that either party shall desire a partition of the aforementioned real property, said party shall give notice of this intent in writing to the other party. Within thirty (30) days of said notice, the party giving notice shall have a fair appraisal of the property made. The party giving notice shall designate a price equal to or greater than the appraised value. The party receiving notice shall have the option within thirty (30) days of either purchasing the interest of the party giving notice in said real prop-

erty, at an amount equal to the fractional interest of the party giving notice in said real property, times the designated price or selling his interest in said real property to the party giving notice for a sum equal to his fractional interest in said real property, times the designated price.

11. Should litigation be instituted to enforce any of the terms of this agreement, the prevailing party shall be entitled to recover a reasonable attorney's fee.

DATED: _____

_____
(Signed) BARBARA ANDERSON

DATED: _____

_____
(Signed) JANE JOHNSON

7

WHEN MARRIAGE RUINS
A LOVE AFFAIR

MANY PEOPLE WILL TELL YOU that getting married ruined a per-
fectly good relationship. There they were, living together bliss-
fully for several happy years. Then, they decided to get married.
Within a short time after that, they split up. For some people,
marriage destroys a relationship.

Some couples can cope with living together very well. Emotionally, intellectually, psychologically, they go along with the
belief that they have an ideal relationship. They are together because they want to be, and, they are often quick to point out,
they "have the freedom to get up and walk out at any time."
Actually, they can't, many of them, because they are tied together psychologically. They need each other and don't really
want to leave. But there is always that thought that they can take
a walk any time they wish.

"Oh, I'm not married—there are no strings on me," one such
free spirit might say casually.

Often, though, the thought that there are no strings is the only reason that some people do not take that walk. They don't leave simply because of the fact that they can if they want to.

Inevitably, many couples who live together later get married. Everything is the same. Nothing is changed—except that the trap has been sprung. The door is closed. Everything is the same, but nothing is the same. Freedom is gone. You have the same life you had before, but "the magic is gone!"

And you can't leave.

For some men—and women—the moment they cannot leave is the moment when they began planning to take that walk at last. Why such things happen is the province of the psychiatrists and other social scientists. Some couples say they "work harder" in a live-together relationship. They'll tell you that marriage is a pattern of lazy habits. The electricity and challenge and anxiety to please are gone. Marriage can become a nothing thing, whereas the live-together relationship always seemed exciting.

For the lawyer, such situations present an even more tangled problem. Before the Marvin decision there was usually little concern about the years a couple lived together before marrying. But now rights have been established for those previously lost years. How important those rights are can be understood in the type of cases just mentioned. Formerly, if a couple lived together for five years and then married—only to divorce in two years—the property and spousal rights were predicated only upon those last two married years. What about the first five years? Under current case law, such a relationship can be treated more like a seven-year marriage.

A person who lived with a partner for several years and then entered into a marriage can hardly argue that he did not intend to share his or her life with that person. Getting married gives greater strength to the property rights, to the premarital rights stemming from those years together before they made it legal.

"We lived together for seven years and were married for one," the wife can argue. "I want my rights for those first seven years, too. He promised me we would share, and he meant it so much that he put a ring on my finger."

Such a plaintiff has a stronger case than one whose relationship terminated without ever having developed into a legal union. Even a short marriage at the end of a long living-together relationship tends to prove an implied contract. A marriage is indicative and supportive of an implied contract to share. It is important, impressive evidence to a court and a jury.

Movie actor Rod Steiger and his wife Sherry went through such a set of circumstances. Rod started living with Sherry in April of 1970.

Sherry, a former Las Vegas dancer, had been married to jockey Leroy Nelson, who died in her arms after an accident at Agua Caliente Race Track in San Diego, California, in 1956. Rod, famous for powerful portrayals in such movies as *On the Waterfront, The Pawnbroker,* and an Academy Award winner for best actor in *In the Heat of the Night,* had been married twice before, to actress Sally Grace in his early, struggling Broadway years, and then from 1959 to 1969 to actress Claire Bloom.

Sherry moved into Rod's beach house in Malibu, now valued at $3.5 million, which was complete with stables for racehorses. Sherry and Rod both have an avid interest in racehorses, and they owned two—Stained Glass and Sister Glass. They lived together until March of 1973, when they got married. The marriage lasted until May of 1978, when they separated. A divorce action followed. So, they had lived together for three years and were married for five. The marriage outlasted the live-together relationship, but not by very much.

The action I filed on behalf of Sherry in Los Angeles County Superior Court dealt with both periods of their life together—the three-year cohabitation and the five-year marriage. One might think that in cases where live-together relationships develop into marriages one could simply ignore the "illegal" years and gain all that was fair and legal from the marriage rights. But, community property rights and the Marvin Doctrine have combined to make that supposition, if it were ever true, false. A pattern has developed in these live-together-first, marry-later cases. The couple live together in loose arrangements, with oral or implied agreements, but when they marry the property-owning spouse draws up a prenuptial agreement stating that he will not share his property with his bride-to-be. Thus, he thinks, the lack of a written agreement protects his property for the period before the marriage, and the written prenuptial agreement protects him afterward.

In *Steiger* v. *Steiger,* it was our position that when Sherry moved in with Rod in April of 1970, they "entered into an oral agreement wherein each agreed that during the time thereafter that the parties lived together as husband and wife, they would combine their skills, efforts, labor and earnings, and would share equally any and all property acquired and accumulated as a result of said skills, efforts, labor and earnings."

The petition continued in language typical of such cases: "That it was further agreed that during the time the parties lived together that Plaintiff (Sherry) and Defendant (Rod) would and did hold themselves out to the general public as husband and wife and Plaintiff would render her services as a companion, homemaker, housekeeper, cook, business advisor and confidante to said Defendant and thereby contribute her skills, efforts, labor and earnings toward the acquisition and accumulation of property."

We also contended that the oral agreement included these points:"That Defendant Steiger would provide for all of Plaintiff's financial support and needs for the rest of her life in the same style and manner that was established during the time the parties lived together, consistent with Defendant Steiger's annual earnings in an amount not at this time known by Plaintiff but believed to be in excess of $600,000 per year.

"That Plaintiff would always be entitled to reside, live in and occupy the residential real property located at . . . Malibu, California."

In other words, Sherry had agreed to move in and live with Rod on his promise that they would share a life together. Among other things, Rod told her specifically that the Malibu house "is yours just as much as mine," and that "I'll never take this house away from you, so Sherry testified."

Our suit identified the "equitable property" Sherry and Rod acquired during the time they lived together through their "skills, efforts, labor and earnings," as an "improved interest" in the Malibu house, furnishings and artwork in the house, interests in the motion pictures *W.C. Fields and Me, F.I.S.T., Love and Bullets, Charley, Wolf Lake, Mussolini, the Last Four Days, The Heroes, Lolly Madonna XXX, Duck You Suckers!* (also released as *Fistful of Dynamite*), plus other properties.

Sherry assumed that they were half-partners in all that was accumulated, and contended she was entitled to half.

Just before they were married, however—practically on the way to the altar—Rod suddenly presented Sherry with a prenuptial agreement to sign. Basically, the agreement—also called an ante-nuptial agreement—declared that any and all property that each one owned would remain his or her separate property.

That prenuptial agreement stated, in part: "Each of the parties hereby acknowledges and agrees that all property of every kind and character, whether real, personal or mixed, and wherever situated, owned or held by either of them at the time of their marriage, or in which either of them shall have, claim or assert any right, title or interest, shall at all times thereafter be the sole and separate property of the party who owns, holds or claims the same, free and clear of any and all claims and interests of the other."

In other words, the agreement stated that whatever was Sherry's remained hers and whatever was Rod's remained his.

Sherry understood this agreement to state that the half of their property that Rod had orally promised her—including the promise that she could live in the Malibu house for the rest of her life—would remain hers. Rod took the position that the agreement meant he owned all the property.

Our argument was that Sherry would never have signed such an agreement if she understood that to be the meaning. Also, we argued that she was under Rod's influence because of the confidential relationship that existed between them and because she reposed "the greatest confidence and trust" in Rod.

She assumed he would treat her fairly.

"She entrusted Defendant Steiger to manage and care for all the joint property acquired and accumulated during the term of their relationship, and to account for all joint property acquired and accumulated through the joint efforts of Plaintiff and Defendant Steiger. By reason of this confidence reposed in Defendant

Steiger, and of which Defendant Steiger was aware, Defendant did retain title, possession, custody and control of the joint property . . .

"By reason of the trust and confidence Plaintiff reposed in Defendant Steiger, Plaintiff relied on Defendant Steiger to perform his agreement with Plaintiff and to disclose fully all other joint property of the parties."

Such were some of the points of petition.

After Sherry's $3-million divorce action was filed against Rod in February of 1978, he produced the ante-nuptial agreement stating that Sherry had waived her community-property rights during the marriage. Los Angeles Superior Court Judge Harry T. Shafer ruled that the 1973 prenuptial (or ante-nuptial) agreement was, indeed, valid and binding.

But, that didn't settle the question.

Even if the prenuptial agreement were valid and Sherry had waived her rights to community property accumulated during the five years of marriage, it did not cover the almost four years they had lived together before they married. Could Sherry share in community property for the years when they lived together even though she could not for the married years? Under the California Supreme Court Marvin decision, she certainly could, it seemed to both me and Harold Rhoden, my cocounsel.

We argued that Rod had made an oral agreement with Sherry when they moved in together in April of 1970 to share equally, and that case law held that oral agreements shall be enforced. Sherry should be able to assert her rights for those years when they lived together. Los Angeles Superior Court Judge Robert Fainer upheld our argument and ruled that Sherry is entitled to assert her rights for those four premarriage years. The written, ante-nuptial agreement, signed when Sherry and Rod married, "certainly doesn't destroy or eliminate or waive any rights."

What Judge Fainer said was that any express or implied promises that Rod had made to Sherry during those years when they lived together could be enforced. What promises had been made?

Well, among other things, Rod had promised Sherry that his Malibu house and grounds were "as much yours as it is mine," and that she could "always live in the house." "I'll never make you leave the house," he had said. That's an express oral promise, we alleged. It should be enforced. If it is enforced, then Rod has given Sherry a life-estate in the house, something worth at least half the estimated $3.5-million value of the house.

And so, we argued, before Sherry and Rod married, she was already part owner of the house to the extent of a life-estate. Then they got married, and Rod drew up a prenuptial agreement declaring that "everything Sherry owns is hers, and everything I own is mine." We also made the following contentions:

If Sherry owned a life interest in the house and all their accumulated property by virtue of an express oral promise made when they lived together, then the prenuptial agreement—which came afterward—merely confirmed it.

The prenuptial agreement did not say that Rod owns the house alone, but that everything he owns remains his and everything that Sherry owns remains hers. Thus, the life-estate in the house that he gave her remains hers under the prenuptial agreement.

Rod's prenuptial agreement, which did not specify individual property but merely declared that "all property of every kind" remains in possession of its owner, was basically meaningless.

If the prenuptial contract had declared that Rod and Sherry agree that his Malibu house shall not be shared but shall remain Rod's own separate property, Sherry would not have signed the agreement.

The prenuptial agreement and the express oral agreement should both be valid, in which case Sherry has a life interest in the house, plus all her other interest in property accumulated during the live-together years.

Another case in which marriage apparently ruined a good relationship involved producer Freddie Fields and his wife, Cherie. Freddie and Cherie lived together for four years before they got married in November of 1976, a month before the Marvin decision was handed down.

As in the Steiger case, Fields drew up a prenuptial agreement for Cherie to sign declaring that all his separate property would remain his and all hers would remain hers.

But Fields listed his house at Malibu and every other property he owned specifically as property not to be shared with Cherie.

When the Fields marriage broke up after only six months, Cherie was unable to claim any of Fields's property that was listed specifically in the prenuptial agreement. Santa Monica Superior Court Judge Raymond Choate ruled at the 1977 divorce trial that the Fields prenuptial agreement was valid, as the Steiger agreement was valid. He held that the prenuptial agreement cut off all of Cherie's property rights for the years they lived together —not by name and not by intention to do so. It cut off the property rights by virtue of the fact that the agreement excluded all of Fields's property by specific description.

In the Steiger case, Sherry Steiger was excluded from an interest in all property that was Rod's separate property, but none of the property was listed specifically.

Sherry Steiger's position was that the property she owned separately—including the life interest in the house—was not described in the agreement as Rod's property. It couldn't be, because he had given it to her. The Marvin decision gave her the right to come into court and prove she had been given a life interest in an express oral agreement.

So, unlike the famed poem of Gertrude Stein that declared, "A rose is a rose is a rose," we see that although one agreement may turn out to smell like a rose, another may not.

An interesting aside to the Steiger case was that Rod initially offered to pay Sherry $1,000 a month temporary support while at the same time he was paying $1,250-a-month support for their two racehorses. Judge Harry Shafer later decided that Steiger should pay Sherry at least as much as he was paying for the horses—and then some: a total of $4,500 a month for temporary support.

Just before the trial, the Steigers agreed to a settlement, thus preventing the court from judicially considering this interesting case.

Here are examples of two prenuptial agreements, one of the Steiger type that is stated in general terms and one of the Fields type that lists all property specifically. Prospective husbands who wish to protect their property in an approaching marriage would do well to make sure they have the right kind of agreement. On the other hand, prospective brides should realize that such agreements, if properly drawn, will effectively waive their rights to any of their new husband's property, as the Fields case proved.

AGREEMENT

This agreement made and entered into at __(Name of City)__, __(Name of State)__, this ____ day of _____, 19____, by and between _____ and _____.

WHEREAS, the parties hereto intend to be married in the near future and desire to settle and determine their respective property rights and interests and other matters related thereto prior to their marriage;

NOW, THEREFORE, the parties hereby agree as follows:

FIRST: Each of the parties hereby acknowledges and agrees that all property of every kind and character, whether real, personal or mixed, and wherever situated, owned or held by either of them at the time of their marriage, or in which either of them shall then have, claim or assert any right, title or interest, shall at all times thereafter be the sole and separate property of the party who owns, holds or claims the same, free and clear of any and all claims and interests of the other.

SECOND: Each of the parties hereby agrees that any property of any kind or character which either of them may acquire after the date of their marriage by gift, devise, bequest or inheritance shall be the sole and separate property of the party acquiring the same, free and clear of any and all claims, rights and interests on the part of the other. The parties further agree that if, after the date of their marriage, either of them shall acquire any property of any kind or character by purchasing the same with his or her separate property or by exchanging the same for all or part of his or her separate property or by obtaining the same in any other manner by the use or conveyance of his or her separate property or funds, such property so acquired shall be the sole and separate property of the party acquiring the same, free and clear of all claims, rights and interests on the part of the other. The parties further agree that any income, dividends, accretions, accumulations or returns accruing from and after the date of their marriage upon or as a result of any of his or her separate property shall be and remain the separate property of the party receiving or acquiring the same, free and clear of any claims, rights and interests on the part of the other.

THIRD: The parties expressly agree that notwithstanding the community property laws of the State of _____ or the laws of any other state, all compensation for personal services of every sort which either of them may receive for services rendered at any time after the date of their marriage shall be the sole and separate property of the party receiving the same, free and clear of any claims, rights and interests on the part of the other, including, but not limited to, any and all community-property rights which each of them would have in the earnings of the other in the absence of this agreement.

FOURTH: Save and except as expressly provided to the contrary in the last will and testament of either party or any codicil thereto, each of the parties does hereby waive, release and relinquish any and all rights to act as executor, executrix, administrator or administratrix of the will or the estate of the other, and all dower, curtesy and similar rights in the real and personal property and the estate of the other, as well as the right to receive a family allowance from the estate of the other and the right to claim a homestead in any real property of the other. Each of the parties does hereby waive, release and relinquish all rights to act as guardian or conservator of the person or the estate of the other.

FIFTH: In the event that any paragraph, provision, clause or phrase contained in this agreement shall be determined or adjudicated void, invalid, illegal, voidable or unenforceable, such determination or ajudication shall not invalidate this agreement, which shall remain in full force and effect with the exception of such void, invalid, illegal, voidable or unenforceable paragraph, provision, clause or phrase.

SIXTH: Each of the parties does hereby acknowledge that he or she, as the case may be, has carefully read all of the terms and provisions contained herein, has been fully advised by his or her attorney as to the significance and effect of all of said terms and provisions, and that he or she is entering into this agreement upon mature consideration, freely and voluntarily, and with full knowledge of all his or her legal rights.

SEVENTH: This agreement contains the entire understanding and agreement of the parties with respect to the within subject matter, and all prior understandings and agreements are hereby merged herein. This agreement may not be altered, amended or modified except in writing signed by both of the parties, and shall be binding upon and inure to the benefit of their respective heirs, administrators, executors and assigns.

IN WITNESS WHEREOF, the parties hereto have hereunto subscribed their names the day and year first above written.

_____

(Signature)

_____

(Signature)

ANTE-NUPTIAL AGREEMENT

THIS AGREEMENT made and entered into this _____ day of _____, 19____, by and between JAMES HENRY ("Husband") and CYNTHIA ROBERTS ("Wife").

WHEREAS said parties contemplate entering into a contract and status of marriage, and;

WHEREAS the said parties are severally seized and possessed of real and personal property in his and her own right, respectively, and;

WHEREAS the parties desire that their marriage shall not in any way change their existing legal rights, or of their heirs, in the real and personal property of each of them;

NOW, THEREFORE, IT IS MUTUALLY AGREED AS FOLLOWS:

1. Neither party hereto, by virtue of the said marriage, shall have or acquire any right, title, interest in or claim to the real or personal estate of the other, but the estate of each shall descend to or vest in his or her heirs at law, legatees or devisees as may be prescribed by his or her Last Will and Testament, by the law then in force, as though no marriage had ever taken place between the said parties.

2. If either party shall mortgage, sell or convey his or her real or personal estate, either in whole or in part, the other party hereto shall, upon demand, at any time and from time to time, join in any and every mortgage, deed of trust, deed of conveyance, or in any other instrument that may be necessary or desirable to make the same effectual; provided, however, that neither party shall be required to assume any personal obligation to pay or discharge any debt or obligation of the other.

3. From and after the date hereof, all wages, salaries and other compensation, or the proceeds thereof, earned or received by Husband from Ajax Widgets, Inc., shall be and remain his separate property and shall not be community property; and from and after the date hereof all wages, salaries, and other compensation, or the proceeds thereof, earned or received by Wife shall be and remain her separate property and shall not be community property.

4. Except as otherwise specifically provided herein, all property, real or personal, owned by Husband as his separate property as of the date hereof, and all property thereafter acquired by him from his separate property or the proceeds thereof, shall be and remains his separate property, and all property, real or personal, owned by Wife as her separate property as of the date hereof, and all property thereafter acquired by her from her separate property or the proceeds thereof, shall be and remain her separate property.

5. This agreement is entered into by the parties hereto with full knowledge on the part of each of the extent and probable value of all of the property or estate of the other, and of all rights that, but for this agreement, would be conveyed by law upon each of them in the property or estate of the other by virtue of the consummation of the said proposed marriage; and the rights of the

respective parties hereto in and to each other's earnings, property and estate, of whatever character the same may be, shall be determined, fixed and settled by this agreement and not otherwise. Attached hereto as Exhibit "A" are financial statements setting forth the assets and liabilities of Husband as of _____, 19____. Husband represents and warrants that Exhibit "A" constitutes a true and correct statement of the nature and extent of his assets and liabilities as of the date hereof. Attached hereto as Exhibit "B" are statements setting forth the assets and liabilities of Wife as of the date hereof. Wife represents and warrants that Exhibit "B" constitutes a true and correct statement of the nature and extent of her assets and liabilities as of the date hereof.

6. The parties hereto agree that, in the event either party shall die prior to the time he had changed his Will so as to acknowledge the fact of his marriage to the other party, nevertheless such Will shall not become invalid thereby in whole or in part, and (except as to rights specifically granted in this agreement) each party agrees that he will assert no claim of any nature whatsoever against the estate of the other party, and further agrees not to oppose the probate of the said Will.

7. Nothing herein contained shall be construed as restricting or waiving the rights of the parties hereunder to file such joint husband-and-wife income tax returns as may be permitted by any applicable state or federal law. Each party agrees, at the request of the other, to execute any and all such proper returns as the other party may request at any time and from time to time during the continuance of the marriage of the parties, and the execution of such joint returns shall in no wise be construed as a waiver of, or in diminution of, any of the provisions of this agreement. Each party agrees to hold the other harmless from (and to pay from his separate property and not from any community property) any and all claims, assessments, deficiencies, interest and/or penalties (as well as attorneys' and accountants' fees, court costs and other related expenses) arising out of any state or federal income tax returns heretofore or hereafter filed by such party or Husband and Wife jointly to the extent such claims, assessments, interest and/or penalties are based upon the failure (or alleged failure) to report income which was or would be the separate property of

such party or based on the disallowance (or attempted disallowance) of deductions, costs, losses or similar items paid, incurred or suffered (or assertedly paid, incurred or suffered) from such party's separate property.

8. Each of the parties waives any right to receive from the estate of the other any widow's or widower's allowance, and any right of dower, curtesy or similar right which either may have under the laws of any state of which the parties, or either of them, may be domiciled.

9. Husband has two children by a former marriage, being Tom Henry, born _____, and Sally Henry, born _____. Wife has a child by a former marriage, being Robert Roberts, born _____. Each party shall provide directly for the support, maintenance and education of his or her children by a former marriage, from his or her separate property. Nothing contained in this agreement shall, however, be construed as absolving either party of his or her legal obligations to support any children of the contemplated marriage.

10. Nothing herein shall be construed as preventing or restricting the right of any party hereto to receive any devise or bequest provided for him by the last will and testament of the other party. Within 30 days after the event of the marriage between the parties, Husband shall transfer to Wife a policy of life insurance on Husband's life in the face amount of _____, and Husband further agrees that for his lifetime (unless Wife shall predecease Husband) he shall make, or shall cause to be made, the necessary premium payments to keep such policy in full force and effect.

11. If Husband and Wife are married and living together at the time of Husband's death, Husband agrees that, upon his death, the residence commonly described as _____ _____ will be transferred to Wife, subject to then existing encumbrances, and Husband will promptly execute a written instrument (Codicil to Will or other appropriate method) to implement his agreement. The provisions of this Paragraph are intended to constitute a contract binding upon Husband and his heirs, executors, administrators and legal representatives and shall be applicable notwithstanding any provision to the contrary in any Will or other testamentary document executed by Hus-

band. Immediately upon Husband's death, and until said property is transferred as provided herein, Wife shall have the right to immediate occupancy of such property without payment of rent.

12. Each of Husband and Wife agrees to indemnify and hold the other harmless from (and to pay out of his separate property and not from any community property) any and all losses, liabilities, costs, expenses, debts, notes, obligations, judgments, causes of action and other claims, including but not limited to attorneys' fees and court costs (hereinafter referred to in the aggregate as "obligations") of every kind, nature or description, whether or not now known or whether now or hereafter arising which obligations are (i) incurred by the indemnifying party before the date of the marriage here contemplated; or (ii) made with respect to, against or by reason of the acquisition, disposition or encumbrancing of property or assets which are such indemnifying party's separate property; or (iii) made with respect to or by reason of actions or activities of such indemnifying party relating to (or for the purpose of) earning, acquiring, disposing of, encumbrancing, retaining or preserving money, assets or property which is, was, would be, or would have been such indemnifying party's separate property.

13. If any part, portion or provision of this agreement shall for any reason be held illegal, invalid or unenforceable, nevertheless all the remaining part, portions and provisions of this agreement shall remain in full force and effect.

14. The present domicile of the parties is in the State of _____. The parties contemplate that their future domicile shall be in the State of _____, and this agreement shall be construed according to, and be controlled by, the laws of the State of _____.

15. This agreement shall bind the parties hereto, their respective heirs, executors, administrators, estates, legal representatives and assigns.

16. Except when the context otherwise requires, the masculine gender shall be construed to include the feminine, and the feminine shall be construed to include the masculine.

17. Each of the parties stipulates that he or she has been represented in the negotiations for and in the preparation of this

agreement by counsel of his or her own choosing; that he or she has read this agreement and has had its contents fully explained to him or her by such counsel, and is fully aware of the contents thereof and of its legal effect.

IN WITNESS WHEREOF, the parties hereto have hereunto set their hands the day and year first above written.

_____	_____
Husband's Signature	Wife's Signature
His Lawyer's Firm	Her Lawyer's Firm
Street Address	Street Address
City, State, Zip	City, State, Zip
Counsel for Husband	Counsel for Wife
By _____	By _____
Lawyer's signature	Lawyer's signature

EXHIBIT A
ASSETS AND LIABILITIES TO
REMAIN AS SEPARATE PROPERTY
OF JAMES HENRY (HUSBAND)

Assets
Cash—$12,500
Notes receivable from Worldwide Gadgets—$35,000
AT&T Stock, shares valued at approx. $25,000
Utopia City Municipal Bonds, valued at approx. $50,000
Ajax Widgets, Inc., located at _____
Family residence at _____
          Book value—$150,000
Apartment building at _____
          Book value—$350,000.
Furnishings and personal property—$25,000
1979 Jaguar, value $18,000
1980 Cadillac, value $15,000
Associated Life Insurance Policy. Face value, $75,000.
          Cash surrender value—$20,000

Liabilities

Notes payable secured by deed of trust on Wandering Lane residence—$30,000.

Notes payable secured by deed of trust on North Ocean Drive apartment building—$75,000.

EXHIBIT B
"ASSETS AND LIABILITIES TO
REMAIN SEPARATE PROPERTY
OF CYNTHIA ROBERTS (WIFE)

Cash—$7,000

Jewelry, clothing and personal effects—$5,000

Furniture and rugs—$30,000

Life Insurance policy, face amount—$100,000

8

WHAT PRICE

GLORIA?

AMONG THE MOST INTRIGUING, perplexing problems brought on by palimony suits is the question of how much a live-in companion is worth. The answer to that question is totally subjective with each couple and also greatly depends upon how much the couple are worth together. It depends, too, upon how much they accumulate together as opposed to how much each had before hooking up with the other.

Recent decisions have established that the services of a homemaker, cook and companion are valuable but have left it up to the individual judge or trier of fact in each case to determine what that value should be. Recently in Redwood City, California, Domestic Relations Commissioner James L. Browning ruled that a divorced wife and mother was entitled to the federal minimum wage of $2.90 per hour for every hour that her former husband made her wait before picking up their three children for court-ordered visits. The mother, Mrs. Sandra Braia, complained to the judge that her estranged husband, Gary, sometimes failed to show up or arrived late to pick up the children, thus causing her to cancel plans or forcing her to hire a baby-sitter. If she couldn't get a sitter, she had to give up extra work as a nurse or cancel recreational activities, which she needed. Commissioner Browning's order presumably cured the husband's erratic arrivals.

On the other hand, Mrs. Susan J. Cropp, twenty-nine, said in a divorce suit against her physician husband, Dr. Craig Cropp, in Minneapolis that she and her parents had helped pay his way through medical school. The wife said she had typed his papers, cleaned the house, cooked his meals and maintained the family car. She figured her contribution at $32,800.

Mrs. Cropp told Judge Donald Barbeau of Hennepin County District Court that her husband put her on a demerit system, and fined her for each demerit. Once, she said, he gave her forty demerits for leaving the patio door open. Susan, who had been married to the demanding doctor for five years, won an uncontested divorce, and the judge awarded her $24,600.

There have been several cases in which a wife worked to put her husband through medical school or law school, only to find herself divorced soon after he graduated. When the abandoned wife so desires, judges have ordered the ex-husband to pay her way through either medical school or law school.

There was a Japanese businessman who paid his wife $24,000 a year—$2,000 a month—for her services.

How do you establish the value of homemaking and companionship? What is the value of a woman who cleans the house, cooks for the man and his children, does the gardening, cleans the pool and/or entertains at social functions for business associates? I argue from the point of view: "What would it cost to do all these things?"

How much would it cost to hire a housekeeper? A cook? A gardener? A governess? A social secretary?

This is a good argument. It is usually acceptable to the courts.

Of course, adding up these separate functions, you can arrive at some lofty figures. You can determine that the woman should be paid $15,000, which might be as much as the man earns. But such figures are offset by how much the woman has already received during the time involved.

In some cases what the woman received might be equal to or more than what she contributed. In the case of producer Freddie Fields and Cherie Lattimer Fields, for example, she had received close to $100,000 in benefits over a three-year period. If she had not been treated so well, she might have received a considerably larger award.

Also, the man can argue that his companionship was of equal value to the woman. In one case, when the woman asked for half of the man's property after a twenty-one-year unmarried cohabitation, he responded that she owed him seventeen years' back rent at $200 a month.

Of course, there has to be something accumulated for there to be something to divide. If a couple lives together for ten years and they accumulate nothing, there is nothing to divide. But if they start out together, and during ten years of living together he builds up a business worth $100,000, then they might have to divide it equally. If the woman helped in the business—or provided some combination of money, services and companionship —the court might very well divide the property.

If the relationship is a mistress-lover situation, in which all she does is paint her toenails and all he does is come by for sex and to give her $200 a week, that is all there is to that. If the promise is, "I'll give you $200 a week for sex," that is prostitution, and nothing more can come of it—even if there is a written contract. That, no doubt, is why members of the world's oldest profession traditionally ask for cash in advance.

The problem of the arrangement being termed prostitution, or some kind of sex-for-pay, clouds any situation in which the sexual acts are crimes in the state in which they occur. As in the case of homosexuals who live together in a state where homosexual acts, even between consenting adults, are a crime, a partner in such a situation may not be able to recover anything, unless she can show enough other elements to indicate that a de facto marriage existed, or that an enforceable promise was made.

That's what happened in the case involving rock star millionaire Peter Frampton and his live-in friend, Penelope McCall.

McCall was married to Frampton's road manager, Mick Brigden in 1973 when she moved in with Frampton. She and Frampton stayed together through 1978, although she remained married to Brigden until 1976. In a palimony suit she filed in Westchester County Supreme Court in New York State, McCall relied on an express oral promise that she said Frampton had made to her. She said that he promised to share his earnings with her in return for her living with him and using her "management expertise" to promote his career. That promise was what induced her to leave her husband and move in with the British-born singer, she argued. Her action sought half of his multi-million-dollar earnings and coownership of his fifty-three acre estate in Croton-on-Hudson north of New York City.

Supreme Court Justice Joseph Gagliardi, however, ruled that McCall had no rights in the situation because the alleged oral contract was based upon "the commission of adultery."

Because McCall was married when she moved in with Frampton and continued to be married for more than three of the years she remained with the singer, she was in the position of the meretricious spouse.

Penelope could make no claims stemming from the adulterous liaison with Frampton because, Justice Gagliardi pointed out, they were engaged in adultery, and adultery is a Class-B misdemeanor in the State of New York.

Parenthetically, it should be pointed out that in virtually all nineteen states that still carry adultery on their books as crimes, the laws are never enforced and have not been in recent memory. Why do these laws remain on the books and why have they not been declared unconstitutional? Because no one is prosecuted under these statutes, the opportunity to challenge them doesn't arise. Most legal experts agree that when one of these statutes is finally challenged in the Supreme Court, these adultery and cohabitation criminal statutes will be put to bed once and for all—paving the way for full recognition of the civil rights of live-ins.

Frampton was also able to show that he and McCall did not hold themselves out as a married couple, that their union produced no children, that they did not file joint income-tax returns or hold property jointly. The union did not amount to a de facto marriage or a common-law marriage, either.

But actually, such elements were beside the point, because Justice Gagliardi ruled in the case, *McCall* v. *Frampton,* that the cohabitation was pure and simple adultery, which "is clearly opposed to sound morality and is based on the illicit association of the parties. Thus, it is void and unenforceable."

The judge again harked back to the "public policy" that discourages adultery and divorce: "It is contrary to the public policy of this state, which recognizes the state of marriage and the protection thereof as essential to the welfare of our society."

As in other cases, the priority was to protect public policy even if the result harmed one of the litigants. That was simply unfortunate.

"This rule is not based on a desire to benefit the party who breached the illegal contract," he noted, "but on a desire to protect the commonweal, the general welfare of society being damaged by the very making of such a contract. By refusing to enforce such a contract and leaving the parties without a legal remedy for breach, society is protected by discouraging the making of contracts contrary to the common good," he concluded.

If there is no criminal or other legal bar to recovery, however, then the questions remain: Is there accumulated property to divide? Is there an agreement? If there is only an oral or implied agreement—the usual situation, because if there were a written agreement chances are that the case would not wind up in court —then the question is how to show it and how to prove the contribution of the non-wage-earning partner.

If a woman takes up with, say, a Picasso, after he has already become a world-famous artist and his paintings are bringing $100,000 each, what is her contribution worth? You might have trouble arguing that a neurosurgeon is a great surgeon because he has a happy home life. One might argue that a brain surgeon—or a diamond cutter—either is skilled or he is not, no matter whom he lives with. Maybe George has already done the same thing for five years while living alone that he still does with consummate skill now that Martha has moved in. For five years when he was alone and for five years when he was with a live-in woman, he went in every day and worked on people's heads. How can you argue that she has made a large contribution with her homemaking skills and companionship?

Well, maybe there are other aspects to the case. Maybe the lawyer can show that George did not do so well financially during those first five years, in spite of his wonderful skill. Maybe entertaining was important to building up that practice. Maybe he did not have much business at first, and was not very social or well connected. You might be able to argue that his live-in woman was charming, socially aware, interesting and helped him eventually develop a lucrative practice—and now he's on the staff of the Menninger Clinic. It can be established that the live-in woman was highly important to him, despite the skill he had all along.

You have to argue particular values. What kind of a wife would Alexandre Dumas have needed so that he could write *The Three Musketeers?* Did he need three inches of tepid incense water and his wife playing a zither beside him? In that situation, her contribution would not be the mere housekeeping but the inspiration, the atmosphere: a synthesis of special values, intangible benefits that significantly helped the creative artist acquire the property. She helped him write better—helped him create—and she should share in the profits of that creative effort.

In 1968, young Cynthia Lang, eighteen years old, cast her lot with a broke, unknown, unwanted rock singer named Vincent Furnier, who changed his name to Alice Cooper. What kind of a career and life did they have at the beginning? Furnier tells about it in his book, *Me, Alice.* He described himself then as "this strange, skinny singer in makeup who kept a coffee can next to the bed to throw up into during the night."

"Cindy stuck," he wrote. "She stuck through that summer when we shared a can of tuna fish between us as our daily food, and she stuck for a good long time after. Cindy said she wasn't much impressed that I'm a rock musician. It never mattered, rich or poor, who I was or what I did. She says I make her laugh."

Furnier goes on to tell of a "penniless Thanksgiving," of getting Cindy pregnant and sending her off to Detroit for an abortion. "I felt bad because she had to drive cross-country with no money, and I was no support at all."

Later, they lived on a farm and a friend "begrudgingly loaned me fifty dollars so Cindy and I could go to the Salvation Army and buy a bedroom ensemble of a stained mattress and three yellow sheets."

Eventually, Cooper's bizarre act caught on and the bad times became good times. "The road separated me from Cindy for months," he wrote. "We started to play at least fifteen dates a month for the next two years, and with traveling time to and from gigs, I was away from Cindy a lot. I missed Cindy, but at the same time I didn't really mind being away from her, in a strange way. I was used to a life-style, of being on the road in bachelor company. If Cindy was the type of girl who needed to be with me constantly, I don't think we would have liked each other for as long as we did. I was wrong in the end. Eventually my life-style and the road led to our break-up."

Significantly, Furnier's acknowledgements in the book thank Cindy Lang "for inspiration."

Lang gave up everything to tend full time to Cooper's personal needs. She became his unlicensed spouse. During their almost seven years together—they split up in 1977—Cooper's fortunes rose from a shared can of tuna fish a day to more than $7 million in assets. What were her contributions worth? I contend she is entitled to share equally in all they accumulated during their seven years together.

Lang's suit against Furnier/Cooper alleged that they entered into an express oral agreement in 1968 in which she would devote her full time and attention to caring for Cooper's personal needs as his companion, homemaker and confidante during the period of time that she lived with him. Cooper, in return, agreed that they would combine their efforts and earnings and share equally in any and all property acquired as a result of their individual or combined efforts . . . and that defendant Furnier would "support plaintiff for her entire lifetime in the same style and manner that was and would be established during the time that the parties lived together."

The couple accumulated profits of $5 million or more through songs, records, concerts and royalties. Cooper's and Lang's income climbed to about $650,000 a year, which, we argue, should entitle Lang to support of about $7,500 a month or $90,000 a year.

As with Sherry Steiger, Cindy was in a relationship of mutual trust and confidence with Furnier, and Furnier controlled all their joint earnings and property.

The *Lang* v. *Furnier* suit clearly indicates a couple who started from scratch together and accumulated millions through nine years of struggle. During those years, Cindy Lang nursed Furnier, sewed costumes, inspired him through penniless days and, as Furnier himself put it, "stuck!"

A different kind of contribution was made by Mary Ann Blackledge, who had a twenty-year relationship with New Orleans supermarket millionaire John G. Schwegmann, Jr., a former Louisiana state senator and a candidate for governor in 1970.

Ms. Blackledge was seventeen and working at the snack counter in one of Schwegmann's stores on Veteran's Memorial Boulevard in suburban New Orleans, when she met the powerful Louisiana businessman-politician in 1958.

In 1966, Ms. Blackledge moved in with Schwegmann and for the next thirteen years they lived as husband and wife. Ms. Blackledge helped rear Schwegmann's children, helped him in every aspect of his business and attended social and political functions as Mrs. Schwegmann.

During the years she was with him, Schwegmann's eight supermarkets earned and were valued at about $60 million.

In a suit filed in the Twenty-Fourth Judicial Court in Jefferson Parish in Gretna, a suburb of New Orleans, cocounsel Bettyanne L. Bussoff and I contended that Ms. Blackledge and Schwegmann entered into a contractual agreement on May 15, 1966, to share their earnings and property equally.

Their relationship went beyond that of a marriage to include business. Ms. Blackledge says she and Schwegmann discussed policy decisions down to the tiniest matters. When he ran for governor, she was introduced everywhere as Mary Ann Schwegmann. Everyone assumed they were married. She was his political ally, confidante, companion, business associate and surrogate mother of his children.

But on May 16, 1978, when she was thirty-eight and had given up twenty years of her life, he suddenly threw her out. "This is a suit that demands equity," and "In the end, they should come out in equal fashion," our petition declared.

There are also cases that involve what we might describe as the "starving wife" and the "gravy-train wife." It's not an unusual story that a couple struggle through lean years together and at about the time they make it—or soon afterward—they split up and the freshly rich and successful man takes up with a new "old lady." Number one was the "starving wife," but number two is on the "gravy train." Many times, in fact, it is only the starving wife and the years of struggle culminating in money and success that enable the man to ever marry or move in with the often glamorous second lady.

Cindy Lang stuck with Furnier in the early starving years, sewing costumes for the act. She stuck with him through thick and thin, and I believe she has a vested interest in the accumulated profits that came later. But it might be more difficult to prove Ms. Lang's contribution if she had moved in after Furnier had already become an established rock star with guaranteed, sold-out bookings and million-plus-selling records.

There are several possible variations on this "starving-wife," "gravy-train-wife" theme.

If the couple does not make a go of it when they are together, if they accumulate nothing, and then split up, and then later with another live-in woman the man hits it big . . . that can be simply tough luck, because, as had been indicated, there has to be something to divide before there can be a division.

If the two of them worked together for several years, however, and during that time the girl worked on the lyrics for some of his songs, it might be a different situation. If they split up, and five years later that lyric she worked on becomes part of a hit song he records, she'd be entitled to claim a share in the profit, unless she had waived these future rights by having reached an earlier settlement.

In the same way, if a company the two started before they split up later becomes very successful and begins to show a lot of profit, the first wife might be able to ask for an increase in her alimony, and/or child support based on the grounds of increased need and changed circumstances.

In some of the live-in cases, there can be a problem with the statute of limitations. If it is a question of a written contract, the time limit to bring action can be up to five years. If the contract is oral or implied, the statute might run out in two years or three, depending upon the state. In the case of a song lyric being used much later, a claim might still be timely if it were filed within the statutory limitation based upon when the song was published or recorded.

As can be readily seen, the possible variables in these cases are almost endless, which is part of the reason why this new field of law is so fascinating.

A live-in who is unwilling to depend upon handouts from the wage-earning spouse or who prefers current real benefits to the promise of future rewards can draw up a straightforward "for hire" agreement. If both parties agree, they can set down exactly what each expects from the other in the matter of property and money sharing. One party may contribute earnings, and the other may contribute companionship and homemaking. Such an agreement would undoubtedly not be as romantic as some might wish, but it would clear up the question of what the live-in party's companionship is really worth. Such an agreement might also preclude any future requests for support, of course. It could have the result of establishing a strictly pay-as-you-go business relationship between an employer and an employee. Indeed, many a real wife might be happy to make such an arrangement. An example of such a contract follows.

FOR-HIRE CONTRACT

AGREEMENT made this ____ day of _____, 19____ between _____, hereinafter referred to as Employer, and _____, hereinafter referred to as Employee:

FIRST
TERM OF EMPLOYMENT

The Employer hereby employs the Employee, and the Employee hereby accepts employment with Employer for ____ months each year, beginning with _____, and ending with _____ of each year, during the years of _____, subject, however, to prior termination of this Agreement as hereinafter provided. During the remainder of each of the aforesaid years, the Employee shall not be in the employ of Employer, and the Employee shall have the right to take other employment with other Employers; Employee shall be exclusively entitled to all compensation received by him for such other employment.

OR

The Employer hereby employs the Employee, and the Employee hereby accepts employment with Employer for a period consisting of the entire lifetime of the Employee, commencing on the ____ day of _____, 19____, subject, however, to prior termination of this agreement as hereinafter provided.

SECOND
DUTIES OF EMPLOYEE

The Employee is hereby hired as _____, and shall work at _____, the _____ of the Employer, located at _____, in _____, and at such other places as may be directed by the Employer. The Employee shall (set forth duties) carefully and accurately, and perform all duties commonly discharged by _____ and such other duties of a similar nature as may be required from time to time by Employer.

THIRD
COMPENSATION OF EMPLOYEE

As compensation for services rendered under this Agreement, the Employee shall be entitled to receive from the Employer a salary of $_____ per year, payable in equal _____ installments of $_____, on the ____ Friday of each week, or the 15th and final days of each month during the period of employment, prorated for any partial employment period.

FOURTH

EMPLOYEE BENEFITS

The Employer agrees to include the Employee in the hospital, surgical and medical benefit plan adopted by the Employer on _____.

OR

The Employer agrees to reimburse the Employee for all medical, dental and hospital bills incurred by Employee for himself or herself. The Employer further agrees to pay such bills directly, rather than to reimburse Employee for payment, on demand from Employee, but only if the bills are submitted in advance to the Employer for his approval. Provided, however, that all such reimbursements or direct payments by the Employer shall be limited to that portion of such bills, if any, which will not be paid by insurance.

FIFTH

REIMBURSEMENT OF EXPENSES INCURRED BY EMPLOYEE

The Employee is authorized to incur reasonable expenses in the carrying out of his or her duties, including _____. The Employer will reimburse the Employee from time to time for all such business expenses, provided that the Employee presents the Employer:

(1) An account book in which the Employee recorded each expenditure at or near the time it was made.

(2) The amount of the expenditure.

(3) The time, place and designation of the type of expenditure.

(4) The business reason for the expenditure.

SIXTH
PROPERTY RIGHTS OF THE PARTIES

On termination of this employment whenever requested by the Employer, the Employee shall immediately deliver to the Employer, all property in his or her possession or under his or her control, belonging to the Employer, including but not limited to

_____.

SEVENTH
OBLIGATIONS OF THE EMPLOYER

The Employer shall indemnify the Employee for all losses sustained by the Employee in direct consequence of the discharge of his or her duties. During the term of this contract, the Employer shall furnish the Employee with (*for example, the use of an automobile, all expenses of operation and maintenance of which are to be paid by the Employer, etc.*)

EIGHTH
OBLIGATIONS OF THE EMPLOYEE

The Employee shall indemnify and save harmless the Employer from all liability from loss, damage or injury to persons or property resulting from the negligence or misconduct of the Employee. The Employee, at all times, during the term of his employment shall keep in full force and effect, at his sole expense, automobile insurance on each automobile owned by him that is used at any time, to carry out any of the duties of his employment.

NINTH
TERMINATION OF EMPLOYMENT

If the Employee willfully breaches or habitually neglects the duties which he or she is required to perform under the terms of this Agreement, the Employer may, at his option, terminate this Agreement, by giving written notice of termination to the Employee without prejudice to any other remedy to which the Employer may be entitled either at law, in equity, or under this Agreement.

This Agreement shall terminate immediately on the occurrence of any one of the following events.

1. The occurrence of circumstances that make the relationship impossible or impractical to be continued.

2. The death of the Employee.

3. The loss by the Employee of legal capacity to contract.

4. The death of the Employer.

5. The loss by the Employer of legal capacity to contract.

6. Willful breach of duty by the Employee in the course of his or her employment, unless waived by the Employer.

7. The habitual neglect by the Employee of his or her employment duties, unless waived by the Employer.

8. The continued incapacity on the part of the Employee to perform his duties, unless waived by the Employer.

9. The willful or permanent breach of the obligations of the Employer to the Employee under this Agreement, unless waived by the Employee.

TENTH
GENERAL PROVISIONS

Any notice to be given hereunder by either party to the other, may be effected either by personal delivery in writing or by mail, registered or certified, postage prepaid, with return receipt requested. Mailed notices shall be addressed to the parties at the addresses appearing in the introductory paragraph of this Agreement, but each party may change his address by written notice in accordance with this paragraph. Notices delivered personally shall be deemed communicated as of actual receipt; mailed notices shall be deemed communicated as of (for example, 5 days after mailing). This Agreement supersedes any agreement and all other agreements, either oral or in writing, between the parties hereto with respect to the employment of the Employee by the Employer and contains all of the covenants and agreements between the parties with respect to such employment in any manner whatsoever. Each party to this Agreement acknowledges that no representations, inducements, promises or agreements, orally or otherwise, have been made by any party, or anyone acting on behalf of any party, which are not provided herein, and that no other agreement, statement or promise not contained in this agreement shall be valid or binding. Any modification of this agreement will be effected only if it is in writing, signed by the party to be charged.

EXECUTED AT _____, _____, on the day and year first above written.

"EMPLOYER"

By: _____

"EMPLOYEE"

By: _____

9

WHAT HATH

MARVIN WROUGHT?

LIKE PANDORA opening the box of the world's ills and sending them abroad to plague mankind, *Marvin* v. *Marvin* caused torment and trouble from the very beginning. It so perplexed the California Supreme Court that it provoked a separate rare opinion by Justice William P. Clark, Jr., which was both concurring *and* dissenting.

Justice Clark basically agreed with the decision that contracts between unmarried cohabitants should be enforced, but then he looked beyond to a foggy sea of future uncertainties.

"The majority opinion properly permits recovery on the basis of either express or implied in-fact agreement between the parties," the justice declared. "These being the issues presented, their resolution requires reversal of the judgment. Here, the opinion should stop."

The opinion did not stop, as we know, and Justice Clark goes on to present his objections to it.

"The court should not attempt to determine all anticipated rights, duties and remedies within every meretricious relationship —particularly in vague terms. Rather, these complex issues should be determined as each arises in a concrete case," he wrote.

"The majority broadly indicates that a party to a meretricious relationship may recover on the basis of equitable principles and in quantum meruit. However, the majority fails to advise us of the circumstances permitting recovery, limitations on recovery, or whether their numerous remedies are cumulative or exclusive. Conceivably, under the majority opinion a party may recover half of the property acquired during the relationship on the basis of general equitable principles, recover a bonus based on specific equitable considerations, and recover a second bonus in quantum meruit."

What the justice pointed out was that an unmarried cohabitant might recover half of the property under an oral or implied contract and also be paid for her services as a companion, housekeeper and cook, whereas a divorcing legal wife who performed such housewifely services is presumed to have performed them out of love and affection and cannot collect for them.

It was this quirk in the decision that caused the *New York Times* to comment that the *Marvin* decision could cause former mistresses in California to receive better treatment than ex-wives in New York!

Justice Clark's concurring/dissenting opinion went on: "The general sweep of the majority opinion raises but fails to answer several questions."

There are six questions that Justice Clark addresses himself to.

"First, because the (California) Legislature specifically excluded some parties to a meretricious relationship from the equal division rule of Civil Code section 4452, is this court now free to create an equal division rule?"

The code allows for the division of community property only for a putative spouse—that is, for a spouse who believed in good faith that he or she had been legally married. Equal division of property between parties of a live-together relationship who know they are not married is inevitable, I believe, and courts in several jurisdictions have granted such division.

"Second, upon termination of the relationship, is it equitable to impose the economic obligations of lawful spouses on meretricious parties when the latter may have rejected matrimony to avoid such obligations?"

This question goes to the heart of the matter for many would-be carefree bachelors and liberated women who have deliberately sidestepped marriage. Justice Clark was wondering if *Marvin* v. *Marvin* wiped out the possibility of a "no strings" relationship even when it was specifically sought by both parties to the relationship. If both parties sign a "nonmarriage agreement" with their eyes open, deliberately stating their preference to avoid marriage and its entanglements, does the *Marvin* decision declare that it cannot be if one party later reneges? Is living together virtually the same as getting married if one of the parties decides it should be?

The question is whether the law will allow a couple to live together without legal entanglements if that is their express desire.

"Third, does not application of equitable principles—necessitating examinations of the conduct of the parties—violate the spirit of the Family Law Act of 1969, designed to eliminate the bitterness and acrimony resulting from the former fault system in divorce?"

There can be no doubt that *Marvin* v. *Marvin* did resurrect the bitter "divorce trial" proceedings, as the trial of the issues in the case demonstrated. It would appear that such trials are inescapable and inevitable under the Marvin decision unless or until laws covering unmarried cohabitation are codified in the several states.

"Fourth, will not application of equitable principles reimpose upon trial courts the unmanageable burden of arbitrating domestic disputes?"

As question three indicates, domestic wrangling in the courts appears inescapable under the Marvin Doctrine.

"Fifth, will not a quantum meruit system of compensation for services—discounted by benefits received—place meretricious spouses in a better position than lawful spouses?"

Justice Clark's final question is:

"Sixth, if a quantum meruit system is to be allowed, does

fairness not require inclusion of all services and all benefits re- gardless of how difficult the evaluation?''

This must surely be the darkest corner of Pandora's box; or, if one thinks of the ills as escaped plagues, it must surely be the most elusive quarry to recapture. Who owns a scale fine enough to measure all the services in a relationship and what each is worth?

Justice Clark's concurring/dissent concludes:

"When the parties of a meretricious relationship show by ex- press or implied in fact agreement they intend to create mutual obligations, the courts should enforce the agreement. However, in the absence of agreement, we should stop and consider the ramifications before creating economic obligations which may vi- olate legislative intent, contravene the intention of the parties, and surely generate undue burdens on our trial courts.

"By judicial overreach, the majority performs a nunc pro tunc marriage, dissolves it, and distributes its property on terms never contemplated by the parties, case law or the legislature.''

Since the California Supreme Court propounded the Marvin decision in December of 1976, the principles have spread rapidly across the land. Some twenty-four states have adopted the Mar- vin decision in one way or another, and I have predicted from the outset that within five years of *Marvin* v. *Marvin* all fifty jurisdic- tions will develop some kind of Marvin Doctrine. It seems to me inevitable simply because a new field of law must of necessity follow the new unmarried life-style that has spread across the nation. The courthouse doors cannot be barred against such a flood of people.

Some of the cases that followed *Marvin* carried the Marvin Doctrine even further than the landmark case. In New Jersey's *Kozlowski* v. *Kozlowski,* for example, the deserted unmarried spouse won support for the rest of her life. In *Carlson* v. *Olson,* a 1977 Minnesota case involving a cohabitation of twenty-one years, a trial court allowed partition of the accumulated property in an amount equal to half, and the Minnesota Supreme Court upheld the ruling. In *Beal* v. *Beal* in Oregon and *McCullon* v. *McCullon* in New York in 1978 the Marvin Doctrine was applied.

The New York case, in Erie County Supreme Court, cited

several other decisions and then pointed to the Marvin decision: "Lastly, California, which has been a front runner in this country, setting forth innovative approaches to social problems in most areas of the law, has recently enunciated a doctrinal change concerning de facto marriages in two landmark decisions which should serve as a guiding beacon for the rest of the country."

In both *Beal* v. *Beal* and *McCullon* v. *McCullon* the courts found that implied contracts existed and should be enforced.

Although some observers decried the Marvin decision, shaking a stern finger of morality and public policy at acceptance of a lifestyle that could undermine society, other cases were developing showing the results of denying the Marvin principles. If accepting Marvin was repugnant to some in that it condoned unmarried cohabitation, what is the result of rejecting the Marvin decision? The Illinois case of Victoria L. Hewitt versus Robert L. Hewitt offers some insight.

As Illinois Supreme Court Justice Robert Underwood wrote in the 1979 opinion, "The issue in this case is whether plaintiff Victoria Hewitt, whose complaint alleges she lived with defendant Robert Hewitt from 1960 to 1975 in an unmarried family-like relationship to which three children have been born, may recover from him 'an equal share of the profits and properties accumulated by the parties' during that period."

Let us examine *Hewitt* v. *Hewitt,* which is a more typical example of unmarried cohabitation than the more spectacular and rarefied cases involving millionaire rock stars and their "old ladies."

Victoria and Robert were both students at Grinnell College in Iowa in 1960 when she became pregnant. Robert told her that he would "share his life, his future earnings and his property" with her, and "told her that they were husband and wife and would live as such, no formal ceremony being necessary," according to her allegations in court papers.

"The parties immediately announced to their respective parents that they were married, and thereafter held themselves out as husband and wife."

Victoria devoted herself to Robert's education, "and his establishment in the practice of pededontia [children's dentistry], obtaining financial assistance from her parents," and putting her payroll checks from her earnings into their common funds.

It seems that Robert, who allegedly had nothing in those student days, eventually achieved annual earnings of $80,000 a year and "accumulated large amounts of property."

During fifteen years together, they were assumed to be husband and wife, became parents of three children and Victoria gave him "every assistance a wife and mother could give, including social activities designed to enhance his social and professional reputation."

In 1975, the relationship broke up and Victoria filed for "divorce." Robert came into court and answered the case of *Hewitt* v. *Hewitt* by denying he was married. Victoria then "admitted that no marriage ceremony had taken place and that the parties have never obtained a marriage license." Although the case was no longer a matrimonial matter, it retained its original citation of *Hewitt* v. *Hewitt*.

Fifteen years together, three children and a holding out that they were married would prove that a common-law marriage existed. But Illinois had outlawed common-law marriage in 1905. The trial court, therefore, dismissed her petition because no marriage existed.

Victoria filed an amended petition, citing the promises Robert had made to her, but the trial court again threw the petition out because "Illinois law and public policy require such claims to be based on a valid marriage."

Victoria carried her suit to the Illinois Fourth District Appellate Court, and the appellate court reversed, citing the Marvin decision. It pointed out that here was a respectable couple in every way. "The parties had outwardly lived a conventional married life, [and] plaintiff's conduct had not 'so affronted public policy that she should be denied any and all relief,' and that plaintiff's complaint stated a cause of action on an express oral contract."

The appellate court went on to say that the Hewitts "had lived 'a most conventional, respectable and ordinary family life,' had 'held themselves out as a married couple for fifteen years,' and 'did not openly flout accepted standards.' "

"The 'single flaw' [was] the lack of a valid marriage," the court concluded.

Here, then, was a couple who would be considered married in a common-law-marriage state, who had in no way paraded an illicit relationship in public, who had held themselves out as married and had produced three children. The relationship qualified as a de facto marriage by any definition and fell within the embrace of the Marvin decision.

The appeals court also noted that the Illinois Marriage and Dissolution of Marriage Act "does not prohibit nonmarital cohabitation" and that the Illinois Criminal Code "makes fornication an offense only if the behavior is open and notorious."

Robert Hewitt, however, appealed to the Illinois Supreme Court. He did not deny paternity of the three children, only that he was married. The question was not support for the children, but of any other sharing. After fifteen years of what was, in effect, a common-law marriage and three children, Hewitt was repudiating Victoria Hewitt as a meretricious spouse—a prostitute.

The Illinois Supreme Court briefly retraced the history of the law in the Land of Lincoln, beginning with *Wallace* v. *Rappleye* in 1882 in which the same court held, "An agreement in consideration of future illicit cohabitation between the plaintiffs is void," which was pure Pontius Pilate. "This is the traditional rule, in force until recent years, in all jurisdictions."

Next, it recalled Corbin's 1962 Restatement of Contracts, which said, "A bargain in whole or in part for or in consideration of illicit sexual intercourse or of a promise thereof is illegal." *Corbin on Contracts* is an accepted authority on contract law by Yale University Law School Professor Arthur Linton Corbin.

The decision continued tracing the line by citing the divisible contract of *Trutalli* v. *Meraviglia* in California that an agreement for sexual intercourse may coexist with a separate business contract agreement without nullifying it.

It quoted *Marvin* that household services are sufficient consideration to form a separate contract and conceded that several states—including Minnesota in *Carlson* v. *Olson* and Oregon in *Beal* v. *Beal*—had concurred.

"The real thrust of plaintiff's argument here is that we should abandon the rule of illegality because of certain changes in societal norms and attitudes," Justice Underwood remarked.

"It is said that because there are so many unmarried cohabitants today the courts must confer a legal status on such relationships.''

Justice Underwood was thinking long thoughts: ''Of substantially greater importance than the rights of the immediate parties is the impact of such recognition upon our society and the institution of marriage. Will the fact that legal rights closely resembling those arising from conventional marriages can be acquired by those who deliberately choose to enter into what have heretofore been commonly referred to as 'illicit' or 'meretricious' relationships encourage formation of such relationships and weaken marriage as the foundation of our family-based society?

''In the event of death shall the survivor have the status of a surviving spouse for purposes of inheritance, wrongful death actions, workmen's compensation, et cetera?''

In at least one case, a live-in spouse did gain possession of a house she had shared after the man died, despite a claim on the property by the man's legal wife. In that 1973 Michigan case, *Tyranski* v. *Piggins,* trucker Alfred P. Lattavo of Canton, Ohio, met cocktail waitress Mrs. Helen Tyranski while traveling in Detroit, Michigan, in 1963. They lived together for four years in Mrs. Tyranski's house, then in an apartment and finally in a house that Lattavo had built for them on Blue Skies Avenue in suburban Livonia. Mrs. Tyranski was married and had two children, but she had been separated from her husband for many years. She contributed $10,000 toward purchase of the home. She also selected the furniture and decorated the house.

In 1967, Lattavo died. In 1969, Mrs. Lattavo found out about the Blue Skies house and claimed it as part of her late husband's estate. Mrs. Tyranski filed suit in Wayne County Circuit Court, and Judge Neal Fitzgerald ruled in Mrs. Tyranski's favor, holding that the meretricious relationship did not preclude enforcement of the oral agreement between Lattavo and Mrs. Tyranski. On appeal, the First District Michigan Court of Appeals affirmed the decision.

Returning to *Hewitt* v. *Hewitt,* Judge Underwood continues, ''And still more importantly, what of the children born of such relationships? What are their support and inheritance rights and by what standards are custody questions resolved?

"What of the sociological and psychological effects upon them of that type of environment? Does not the recognition of legally enforceable property and custody rights emanating from non-marital cohabitation in practical effect equate with the legalization of Common Law marriage—at least in the circumstances of this case?

"And, in summary, have the increasing numbers of unmarried cohabitants and changing mores of our society reached the point at which the general welfare of the citizens of this state is best served by a return to something resembling the judicially created Common Law Marriage our legislature outlawed in 1905?"

Judge Underwood thus admirably sums up the legal situation presented by today's "Brave New World" life-style. What, indeed, is to be done? It might be suggested that there are, basically, three classes of couples.

1. The legally married.

2. The couples who can be declared married under the common law.

3. The unmarried couples who just live together, and may be considered beyond the law.

The object, of course, is to bring order to these classes so that they may be sorted out as either married or not married, within the law or outside of it. The great, gray area that is not quite either one is vexing to the orderliness of the law.

As we have seen, the courts have tried to straddle this problem. In *Marvin* v. *Marvin*, the court suggested that "past decisions hover over the issue in the somewhat wispy form of a Chagall painting."

Justice Underwood hovers briefly over *Hewitt* v. *Hewitt*. He does not accept the idea that couples can live together in a relationship involving divisible contracts—one a business agreement and one a sexual agreement. To believe this is possible is to display "naivete," he remarks. One cannot believe "the assertion that there are involved in these relationships contracts separate and independent from the sexual activity, [or] the assumption that those contracts would have been entered into or would continue without that activity."

Such unions, therefore, are basically sexual unions, Justice

Underwood concludes, and recognizing them creates a status somewhere between legal marriage and the outcasts.

"The issue, realistically," he says, "is whether it is appropriate for this court to grant a legal status to a private arrangement substituting for the institution of marriage sanctioned by the state."

He does not believe it is realistic, as in *Marvin* v. *Marvin*, to treat such sexual cases as pure contract law, either. "The issue of unmarried cohabitants' property rights . . . cannot appropriately be characterized solely in terms of contract law, nor is it limited to considerations of equality or fairness as between the parties of such relationships. There are major public policy questions involved in determining whether, under what circumstances, and to what extent it is desirable to accord some type of legal status to claims arising from such relationships."

The judge suggests that if some kind of legal status is to be conferred on unmarried cohabitants, "it would seem more candid to acknowledge the return of varying forms of Common Law Marriage." In his opinion and thus in the opinion of the Illinois Supreme Court, the appellate division's reversal had "the practical effect" of reinstating common-law marriage.

Neither the Illinois Supreme Court nor the California Supreme Court in *Marvin* v. *Marvin* wished to bring back common-law marriage.

Without common-law marriage, Victoria Hewitt's case was doomed in Illinois. The Illinois Supreme Court ruled that she had no standing as a wife and that her suit for a share in her "husband's" property was denied, even though it admitted that her "claims are [not] totally devoid of merit."

The court had this to say about a return of common-law marriage:

"The question whether change is needed in the law governing the rights of parties in this delicate area of marriage-like relationships involves evaluations of sociological data and alternatives we believe best suited to the superior investigative and fact-finding facilities of the legislative branch in the exercise of its traditional authority to declare public policy in the domestic relations field."

The Illinois State Legislature must decide if Illinois is to bring back common-law marriage.

Hewitt v. *Hewitt,* which demonstrates the injustice of denying all rights to meretricious spouses in family types of relationships, is a giant step backward, of course. But it does sharpen the focus of the growing, persistent problem of unmarried couples and how to find equity.

The live-togethers are not going to go away. Case law or legislation will develop in each state to handle the multitude of persons who do live together and the problems that arise from their relationships. The cases that will result are bound to be as varied as the possible combinations of litigants: there will be those prudent couples who keep their houses in order and come through without difficulty; there will be others who will create legal hornets' nests of cohabitations. I can only urge those who contemplate unwedded bliss to consider their options, survey the law, draw up fair and realistic agreements when possible and keep in mind that the human condition is an inexact but exciting art form.

10

MARVIN v.

MARVIN

[L.A. No. 30520. Dec. 27, 1976.]

MICHELLE MARVIN,
Plaintiff and Appellant, v.
LEE MARVIN,
Defendant and Respondent.

SUMMARY

A woman brought an action against a man with whom she had lived for approximately six years, in which she alleged that she and defendant entered into an oral agreement that during the time they lived together they would combine their efforts and earnings and share equally the property accumulated through their individual or combined efforts, and that plaintiff would render services to defendant as companion, housemaker, housekeeper and cook, give up her career as an entertainer and singer, and that defendant would provide for all her financial support for the rest of her life. Plaintiff further alleged that later she was forced to leave defendant's household at his request, he refused to pay any further support to her and refused to recognize that she had any interest in the property accumulated while they were living together. Plaintiff prayed for declaratory relief, asking the court to determine her contract and property rights, and also to impose a constructive trust upon one-half of the property acquired during the course of the relationship. The trial court denied plaintiff's motion to amend her complaint to allege that she and defendant affirmed their agreement after defendant's divorce became final, and thereafter granted defendant's motion for judgment on the pleadings. (Superior Court of Los Angeles County, No. C-23303, William A. Munnell, Judge.)

The Supreme Court reversed and remanded for further proceedings. The court held the terms of the contract as alleged by plaintiff did not rest upon any unlawful consideration, that it furnished a suitable basis upon which the trial court could render declaratory relief, and the trial court therefore erred in granting defendant's motion for judgment on the pleadings. The court held generally that while the provisions of the Family Law Act do not govern the distribution of property acquired during a nonmarital relationship, and such a relationship remains subject solely to judicial decision, the courts should enforce express contracts between nonmarital partners except to the extent that the contract is explicitly founded on the consideration of meretricious sexual services. The court further held that in the absence of an express contract, the court should inquire into the conduct of the parties to determine whether that conduct demonstrates an implied contract, agreement of partnership or joint venture, or some other tacit understanding between the parties, and that courts may also employ the doctrine of quantum meruit, or equitable remedies such as constructive or resulting trusts, when warranted by the facts of the case, and that plaintiff's complaint could be amended

to state a cause of action founded on theories of implied contract
or equitable relief. (Opinion by Tobriner, J., with Wright, C. J.,
McComb, Mosk, Sullivan and Richardson, J.J., concurring. Separate concurring and dissenting opinion by Clark, J.)

Classified to California Digest of Official Reports, 3d Series

(1) Appellate Review § 136—Review—Presumptions—Pleadings.—On appeal from a judgment rendered for defendant on the
pleadings, the appellate court must accept the allegations of plaintiff's complaint as true, determining whether such allegations
state, or can be amended to state, a cause of action.

(2) Pleading § 72—Time to Amend—At Trial.—In a civil action, no error was committed by the trial court in denying plaintiff's motion, made on the opening day set for trial, seeking leave
to file a proposed amended complaint which would have added
two counts and a new defendant to the action, in the absence of
a showing of a clear abuse of discretion.

(3a, 3b) Dissolution of Marriage; Separation § 78—Property
Settlement Agreements, Stipulations, and Contracts—Effect and
Enforcement—Nonmarital Relationship.—A complaint filed by
a woman against a man with whom she had lived for approximately six years, alleging that she and defendant made an oral
agreement that during the time they lived together they would
combine their efforts and earnings and share equally the property
they accumulated, and that plaintiff would render services to defendant as companion, housemaker, housekeeper and cook, give
up her career as an entertainer and singer, and that defendant
would provide her financial support for the rest of her life, but
that defendant later forced her to leave his household and refused
to pay any further support to her or to recognize her in the property accumulated while they were living together, stated a cause
of action for breach of an express contract whose terms as alleged
did not rest on any unlawful consideration, and the trial court
therefore erred in granting defendant's motion for judgment on
the pleadings. Adults who voluntarily live together and engage in

sexual relations are nonetheless as competent as any other persons to contract respecting their earnings and property rights, and so long as their agreement does not rest upon any illicit meretricious consideration, they may order their economic affairs as they choose, and no policy precludes the courts from enforcing such agreements.

[See Cal.Jur.3d, Family Law, § 780; Am.Jur.2d, Husband and Wife, § 276.]

(4) Dissolution of Marriage; Separation § 78—Property Settlement Agreements, Stipulations, and Contracts—Effect and Enforcement—Nonmarital Relationship.—The fact that a man and woman live together without marriage, and engage in a sexual relationship, does not in itself invalidate agreements between them relating to their earnings, property, or expenses. Neither is such an agreement invalid merely because the parties may have contemplated the creation or continuation of a nonmarital relationship when they entered into it. Agreements between nonmarital partners fail only to the extent that they rest upon an explicit consideration of meretricious sexual services. (Disapproving *Heaps* v. *Toy* (1942) 54 Cal.App.2d 178 [128 P.2d 813], to the extent it held a support agreement between nonmarital partners unenforceable as contrary to good morals.)

(5) Dissolution of Marriage; Separation § 78—Property Settlement Agreements, Stipulations, and Contracts—Effect and Enforcement—Nonmarital Relationship.—A property and support agreement between a man and woman living in a nonmarital relationship was not violative of public policy by impairing the community property rights of the man's lawful wife, where the wife had the opportunity to assert her community property rights in a divorce action in which her interest was fixed and limited by decrees, and the enforcement of the nonmarital agreement against property awarded to the man by the divorce decree would thus not impair any right of the wife. Furthermore, an improper transfer of community property is not void *ab initio*, but merely voidable at the instance of the aggrieved spouse.

(6) Dissolution of Marriage; Separation § 78—Property Settlement Agreement, Stipulations, and Contract—Effect and Enforcement—Nonmarital Relationship.—Civ. Code, § 5134,

providing that all contracts for marriage settlement must be in writing, did not bar enforcement of an oral agreement for support and property division between a man and woman living together in a nonmarital relationship, since a marriage settlement is an agreement in contemplation of marriage in which each party agrees to release or modify the property rights which would otherwise arise from the marriage, while the contract between the man and woman did not fall within that definition.

(7) Dissolution of Marriage; Separation § 78—Property Settlement Agreements, Stipulations, and Contracts—Effect and Enforcement—Nonmarital Relationship.—Civ. Code, § 43.5, providing that no cause of action arises for breach of a promise of marriage, is not reasonably susceptible to the interpretation that property pooling and support agreements between nonmarital partners, which are not part of or accompanied by promise of marriage, are barred by the statute.

(8a, 8b) Dissolution of Marriage; Separation § 78—Property Settlement Agreement, Stipulations, and Contracts—Effect and Enforcement—Nonmarital Relationship—Equitable Relief.—A complaint by a woman against a man with whom she had lived for approximately six years, alleging that she and defendant entered into an oral agreement that during the time they lived together they would share equally the property accumulated, and that plaintiff would render services to defendant as companion, housemaker, housekeeper and cook, give up her career as an entertainer and singer, and that defendant would provide for all her financial support for the rest of her life, but that defendant thereafter forced her to leave his home and repudiated the agreement, could be amended to state a cause of action founded on theories of implied contract or equitable relief, in addition to a cause of action for breach of an express contract, and the trial court therefore erred in granting defendant's motion for judgment on the pleadings. Courts may look to a variety of remedies in order to protect the lawful expectations of parties to a nonmarital relationship, and may inquire into the conduct of the parties to determine whether it demonstrates an implied contract or implied agreement of partnership or joint venture, or some other tacit understanding, and may, when appropriate, employ principles of constructive trust. Moreover, a nonmarital partner may recover in quantum meruit for the reasonable value of household services rendered, less the reasonable value of support received, if it can be shown that services were rendered with the expectation of monetary reward.

(9) Dissolution of Marriage; Separation § 48—Division of Community and Quasi-community Property—Family Law Act —Nonmarital Relationship.—The Family Law Act does not require an equal division of property accumulated in nonmarital actual family relationships, as no language in the act addresses the property rights of nonmarital partners, and nothing in the legislative history of the act suggests that the Legislature considered that subject, which prior to the act had been fixed entirely by judicial decision.

COUNSEL

Marvin M. Mitchelson, Donald N. Woldman, Robert M. Ross, Fleishman, McDaniel, Brown & Weston and David M. Brown for Plaintiff and Appellant.

Jettie Pierce Selvig, Ruth Miller and Suzie S. Thorn as Amici Curiae on behalf of Plaintiff and Appellant.

Goldman & Kagon, Mark A. Goldman and William R. Bishin for Defendant and Respondent.

Herma Hill Kay, John Sutter, Doris Brin Walker and Treuhaft, Walker, Nawi & Hendon as Amici Curiae on behalf of Defendant and Respondent.

Isabella H. Grant and Livingston, Grant, Stone & Shenk as Amici Curiae.

OPINION

TOBRINER, J.—During the past 15 years, there has been a substantial increase in the number of couples living together with-

out marrying.[1] Such nonmarital relationships lead to legal controversy when one partner dies or the couple separates. Courts of
Appeal, faced with the task of determining property rights in such
cases, have arrived at conflicting positions: two cases (*In re Marriage of Cary* (1973) 34 Cal.App.3d 345 [109 Cal.Rptr. 862]; *Estate of Atherley* (1975) 44 Cal.App.3d 758 [119 Cal.Rptr.41]) have
held that the Family Law Act (Civ. Code, § 4000 et seq.) requires
division of the property according to community property principles, and one decision (*Beckman* v. *Mayhew* (1975) 49
Cal.App.3d 529 [122 Cal.Rptr. 604]) has rejected that holding. We
take this opportunity to resolve that controversy and to declare
the principles which should govern distribution of property acquired in a nonmarital relationship.

We conclude: (1) The provisions of the Family Law Act do not
govern the distribution of property acquired during a nonmarital
relationship; such a relationship remains subject solely to judicial
decision. (2) The courts should enforce express contracts between nonmarital partners except to the extent that the contract
is explicitly founded on the consideration of meretricious sexual
services. (3) In the absence of an express contract, the courts
should inquire into the conduct of the parties to determine
whether that conduct demonstrates an implied contract, agreement of partnership or joint venture, or some other tacit understanding between the parties. The courts may also employ the
doctrine of quantum meruit, or equitable remedies such as constructive or resulting trusts, when warranted by the facts of the
case.

In the instant case plaintiff and defendant lived together for
seven years without marrying; all property acquired during this
period was taken in defendant's name. When plaintiff sued to
enforce a contract under which she was entitled to half the property and to support payments, the trial court granted judgment on
the pleadings for defendant, thus leaving him with all property
accumulated by the couple during their relationship. Since the
trial court denied plaintiff a trial on the merits of her claim, its

---

[1] "The 1970 census figures indicate that today perhaps eight times as many
couples are living together without being married as cohabited ten years ago."
(Comment, *In re Cary: A Judicial Recognition of Illicit Cohabitation* (1974) 25
Hastings L.J. 1226.)

decision conflicts with the principles stated above, and must be reversed.

1. *The factual setting of this appeal.*

(1) Since the trial court rendered judgment for defendant on the pleadings, we must accept the allegations of plaintiff's complaint as true, determining whether such allegations state, or can be amended to state, a cause of action. (See *Sullivan* v. *County of Los Angeles* (1974) 12 Cal.3d 710, 714–715, fn. 3 [117 Cal.Rptr. 241, 527 P.2d 865]; 4 Witkin, Cal. Procedure (2d ed. 1971) pp. 2817–2818.) We turn therefore to the specific allegations of the complaint.

Plaintiff avers that in October of 1964 she and defendant "entered into an oral agreement" that while "the parties lived together they would combine their efforts and earnings and would share equally any and all property accumulated as a result of their efforts whether individual or combined." Furthermore, they agreed to "hold themselves out to the general public as husband and wife" and that "plaintiff would further render her services as a companion, homemaker, housekeeper and cook to . . . defendant."

Shortly thereafter plaintiff agreed to "give up her lucrative career as an entertainer [and] singer" in order to "devote her full time to defendant . . . as a companion, homemaker, housekeeper and cook"; in return defendant agreed to "provide for all of plaintiff's financial support and needs for the rest of her life."

Plaintiff alleges that she lived with defendant from October of 1964 through May of 1970 and fulfilled her obligations under the agreement. During this period the parties as a result of their efforts and earnings acquired in defendant's name substantial real and personal property, including motion picture rights worth over $1 million. In May of 1970, however, defendant compelled plaintiff to leave his household. He continued to support plaintiff until November of 1971, but thereafter refused to provide further support.

On the basis of these allegations plaintiff asserts two causes of action. The first, for declaratory relief, asks the court to determine her contract and property rights; the second seeks to impose a constructive trust upon one half of the property acquired during the course of the relationship.

Defendant demurred unsuccessfully, and then answered the complaint. (2) (See fn.2). Following extensive discovery and pretrial proceedings, the case came to trial.[2] Defendant renewed his attack on the complaint by a motion to dismiss. Since the parties had stipulated that defendant's marriage to Betty Marvin did not terminate until the filing of a final decree of divorce in January 1967, the trial court treated defendant's motion as one for judgment on the pleadings augmented by the stipulation.

After hearing argument the court granted defendant's motion and entered judgment for defendant. Plaintiff moved to set aside the judgment and asked leave to amend her complaint to allege that she and defendant reaffirmed their agreement after defendant's divorce was final. The trial court denied plaintiff's motion, and she appealed from the judgment.

---

[2] When the case was called for trial, plaintiff asked leave to file an amended complaint. The proposed complaint added two causes of action for breach of contract against Santa Ana Records, a corporation not a party to the action, asserting that Santa Ana was an alter ego of defendant. The court denied leave to amend, and plaintiff claims that the ruling was an abuse of discretion. We disagree; plaintiff's argument was properly rejected by the Court of Appeal in the portion of its opinion quoted below.

No error was committed in denial of plaintiff's motion, made on the opening day set for trial, seeking leave to file a proposed amended complaint which would have added two counts and a new defendant to the action. As stated by plaintiff's counsel at the hearing, "[T]here is no question about it that we seek to amend the Complaint not on the eve of trial but on the day of trial."

In *Hayutin* v. *Weintraub*, 207 Cal.App.2d 497 [24 Cal.Rptr. 761], the court said at pages 508–509 in respect to such a motion that had it been granted, it "would have required a long continuance for the purpose of canvassing wholly new factual issues, a redoing of the elaborate discovery procedures previously had, all of which would have imposed upon defendant and his witnesses substantial inconvenience . . . and upon defendant needless and substantial additional expense. . . . The court did not err in denying leave to file the proposed amended complaint." (See also: *Nelson* v. *Specialty Records, Inc.*, 11 Cal.App.3d 126, 138–139 [89 Cal.Rptr. 540]; *Moss Estate Co.* v. *Adler*, 41 Cal.2d 581, 585 [261 P.2d 732]; *Vogel* v. *Thrifty Drug Co.*, 43 Cal.2d 184, 188 [272 P.2d 1].) "The ruling of the trial judge will not be disturbed upon appeal absent a showing by appellant of a clear abuse of discretion. [Citations.]" (*Nelson* v. *Specialty Records, Inc.*, *supra*, 11 Cal.App.3d at p. 139.) No such showing here appears.

2. (3a) *Plaintiff's complaint states a cause of action for breach of an express contract.*

In *Trutalli* v. *Meraviglia* (1932) 215 Cal. 698 [12 P.2d 430] we established the principle that nonmarital partners may lawfully contract concerning the ownership of property acquired during the relationship. We reaffirmed this principle in *Vallera* v. *Vallera* (1943) 21 Cal.2d 681, 685 [134 P.2d 761], stating that "If a man and woman [who are not married] live together as husband and wife under an agreement to pool their earnings and share equally in their joint accumulations, equity will protect the interests of each in such property."

In the case before us plaintiff, basing her cause of action in contract upon these precedents, maintains that the trial court erred in denying her a trial on the merits of her contention. Although that court did not specify the ground for its conclusion that plaintiff's contractual allegations stated no cause of action,[3] defendant offers some four theories to sustain the ruling; we proceed to examine them.

Defendant first and principally relies on the contention that the alleged contract is so closely related to the supposed "immoral" character of the relationship between plaintiff and himself that the enforcement of the contract would violate public policy.[4] He

[3] The colloquy between court and counsel at argument on the motion for judgment on the pleadings suggests that the trial court held the 1964 agreement violated public policy because it derogated the community property rights of Betty Marvin, defendant's lawful wife. Plaintiff, however, offered to amend her complaint to allege that she and defendant reaffirmed their contract after defendant and Betty were divorced. The trial court denied leave to amend, a ruling which suggests that the court's judgment must rest upon some other ground than the assertion that the contract would injure Betty's property rights.

[4] Defendant also contends that the contract was illegal because it contemplated a violation of former Penal Code section 269a, which prohibited living "in a state of cohabitation and adultery." (§ 269a was repealed by Stats. 1975, ch. 71, eff. Jan. 1, 1976.) Defendant's standing to raise the issue is questionable because he alone was married and thus guilty of violating section 269a. Plaintiff, being unmarried could neither be convicted of adulterous cohabitation nor of aiding and abetting defendant's violation. (See *In re Cooper* (1912) 162 Cal. 81, 85–86 [121 P. 318].)

The numerous cases discussing the contractual rights of unmarried couples have drawn no distinction between illegal relationships and lawful nonmarital relationships. (Cf. *Weak* v. *Weak* (1962) 202 Cal.App.2d 632, 639 [21 Cal.Rptr. 9] (bigamous marriage).) Moreover, even if we were to draw such a distinction—a

points to cases asserting that a contract between nonmarital partners is unenforceable if it is "involved in" an illicit relationship
(see *Shaw* v. *Shaw* (1964) 227 Cal.App.2d 159, 164 [38 Cal.Rptr.
520] (dictum); *Garcia* v. *Venegas* (1951) 106 Cal.App.2d 364, 368
[235 P.2d 89] (dictum), or made in "contemplation" of such a
relationship (*Hill* v. *Estate of Westbrook* (1950) 95 Cal.App.2d
599, 602 [213 P.2d 727]; see *Hill* v. *Estate of Westbrook* (1952) 39
Cal.2d 458, 460 [247 P.2d 19]; *Barlow* v. *Collins* (1958) 166
Cal.App.2d 274, 277 [333 P.2d 64] (dictum); *Bridges* v. *Bridges*
(1954) 125 Cal.App.2d 359, 362 [270 P.2d 69] (dictum)). A review
of the numerous California decisions concerning contracts between nonmarital partners, however, reveals that the courts have
not employed such broad and uncertain standards to strike down
contracts. The decisions instead disclose a narrower and more
precise standard: a contract between nonmarital partners is
unenforceable only *to the extent* that it *explicitly* rests upon
the immoral and illicit consideration of meretricious sexual
services.

In the first case to address this issue, *Trutalli* v. *Meraviglia,*
supra, 215 Cal. 698, the parties had lived together without marriage for 11 years and had raised two children. The man sued to
quiet title to land he had purchased in his own name during this
relationship; the woman defended by asserting an agreement to
pool earnings and hold all property jointly. Rejecting the assertion of the illegality of the agreement, the court stated that "The
fact that the parties to this action at the time they agreed to invest
their earnings in property to be held jointly between them were
living together in an unlawful relation, did not disqualify them
from entering into a lawful agreement with each other, so long as
such immoral relation was not made *a consideration* of their
agreement." (Italics added.) (215 Cal. at pp. 701–702.)

In *Bridges* v. *Bridges, supra,* 125 Cal.App.2d 359 [270 P.2d 69],
both parties were in the process of obtaining divorces from their
erstwhile respective spouses. The two parties agreed to live together, to share equally in property acquired, and to marry when

largely academic endeavor in view of the repeal of section 269a—defendant probably would not benefit; his relationship with plaintiff continued long after his
divorce became final, and plaintiff sought to amend her complaint to assert that
the parties reaffirmed their contract after the divorce.

their divorces became final. The man worked as a salesman and used his savings to purchase properties. The woman kept house, cared for seven children, three from each former marriage and one from the nonmarital relationship, and helped construct improvements on the properties. When they separated, without marrying, the court awarded the woman one-half the value of the property. Rejecting the man's contention that the contract was illegal, the court stated that: "Nowhere is it expressly testified to by anyone that there was anything in the agreement for the pooling of assets and the sharing of accumulations that contemplated meretricious relations as any part of the consideration or as any object of the agreement." (125 Cal.App.2d at p. 363.)

Croslin v. *Scott* (1957) 154 Cal.App.2d 767 [316 P.2d 755] reiterates the rule established in *Trutalli* and *Bridges*. In *Croslin* the parties separated following a three-year nonmarital relationship. The woman then phoned the man, asked him to return to her, and suggested that he build them a house on a lot she owned. She agreed in return to place the property in joint ownership. The man built the house, and the parties lived there for several more years. When they separated, he sued to establish his interest in the property. Reversing a nonsuit, the Court of Appeal stated that "The mere fact that parties agree to live together in meretricious relationship does not necessarily make an agreement for disposition of property between them invalid. It is only when the property agreement is made in connection with the other agreement, or the illicit relationship is made a consideration of the property agreement, that the latter becomes illegal." (154 Cal.App.2d at p. 771.)

Numerous other cases have upheld enforcement of agreements between nonmarital partners in factual settings essentially indistinguishable from the present case. (*In re Marriage of Foster* (1974) 42 Cal.App.3d 577 [117 Cal.Rptr. 49]; *Weak* v. *Weak, supra,* 202 Cal.App.2d 632, 639; *Ferguson* v. *Schuenemann* (1959) 167 Cal.App.2d 413 [334 P. 2d 668]; *Barlow* v. *Collins, supra,* 166 Cal.App.2d 274, 277-278; *Ferraro* v. *Ferraro* (1956) 146 Cal.App.2d 849 [304 P.2d 168]; *Cline* v. *Festersen* (1954) 128 Cal.App.2d 380 [275 P.2d 149]; *Profit* v. *Profit* (1953) 117 Cal.App.2d 126 [255 P.2d 25]; *Garcia* v. *Venegas, supra,* 106 Cal.App.2d 364; *Padilla* v. *Padilla* (1940) 38 Cal.App.2d 319 [100

P.2d 1093]; *Bacon* v. *Bacon* (1937) 21 Cal.App.2d 540 [69 P.2d 884].)[5]

Although the past decisions hover over the issue in the somewhat wispy form of the figures of a Chagall painting, we can abstract from those decisions a clear and simple rule. (4) The fact that a man and woman live together without marriage, and engage in a sexual relationship, does not in itself invalidate agreements between them relating to their earnings, property, or expenses. Neither is such an agreement invalid merely because the parties may have contemplated the creation or continuation of a nonmarital relationship when they entered into it. Agreements between nonmarital partners fail only to the extent that they rest upon a consideration of meretricious sexual services. Thus the rule asserted by defendant, that a contract fails if it is "involved in" or made "in contemplation" of a nonmarital relationship, cannot be reconciled with the decisions.

The three cases cited by defendant which have *declined* to enforce contracts between nonmarital partners involved consideration that *was* expressly founded upon an illicit sexual services. In *Hill* v. *Estate of Westbrook, supra,* 95 Cal.App.2d 599, the woman promised to keep house for the man, to live with him as man and wife, and to bear his children; the man promised to provide for her in his will, but died without doing so. Reversing a judgment for the woman based on the reasonable value of her services, the Court of Appeal stated that "the action is predicated upon a claim which seeks, among other things, the reasonable value of living with decedent in meretricious relationship and bearing him two children . . . The law does not award compen-

---

[5] Defendant urges that all of the cited cases, with the possible exception of *In re Marriage of Foster, supra,* 42 Cal.App.3d 577 and *Bridges* v. *Bridges, supra,* 125 Cal.App.2d 359, can be distinguished on the ground that the partner seeking to enforce the contract contributed either property or services additional to ordinary homemaking services. No case, however, suggests that a pooling agreement in which one partner contributes only homemaking services is invalid, and dictum in *Hill* v. *Estate of Westbrook, supra,* 95 Cal.App.2d 599, 603 [213, P.2d 727] states the opposite. A promise to perform homemaking services is, of course, a lawful and adequate consideration for a contract (see *Taylor* v. *Taylor* (1954) 66 Cal.App.2d 390, 398 [152 P.2d 480])—otherwise those engaged in domestic employment could not sue for their wages—and defendant advances no reason why his proposed distinction would justify denial of enforcement to contracts supported by such consideration. (See *Tyranski* v. *Piggins* (1973) 44 Mich.App. 570 [205 N.W.2d 595, 597].)

sation for living with a man as a concubine and bearing him children . . . As the judgment is at least in part, for the value of the
claimed services for which recovery cannot be had, it must be
reversed." (95 Cal.App.2d at p. 603.) Upon retrial, the trial court
found that it could not sever the contract and place an independent value upon the legitimate services performed by claimant.
We therefore affirmed a judgment for the estate. (*Hill* v. *Estate
of Westbrook* (1952) 39 Cal.2d 458 [247 P. 2d 19].)

In the only other cited decision refusing to enforce a contract,
Updeck v. *Samuel* (1954) 123 Cal.App.2d 264 [266 P. 2d 822], the
contract "was based on the consideration that the parties live
together as husband and wife." (123 Cal.App.2d at p. 267.)
Viewing the contract as calling for adultery, the court held it
illegal.[6]

The decisions in the *Hill* and *Updeck* cases thus demonstrate
that a contract between nonmarital partners, even if expressly
made in contemplation of a common living arrangement, is invalid only if sexual acts form an inseparable part of the consideration for the agreement. In sum, a court will not enforce a
contract for the pooling of property and earnings if it is explicitly
and inseparably based upon services as a paramour. The Court
of Appeal opinion in *Hill,* however, indicates that even if sexual
services are part of the contractual consideration, any *severable*
portion of the contract supported by independent consideration
will still be enforced.

The principle that a contract between nonmarital partners will
be enforced unless expressly and inseparably based upon an illicit

---

[6] Although not cited by defendant, the only California precedent which sup-
ports his position is *Heaps* v. *Toy* (1942) 54 Cal.App.2d 178 [128 P.2d 813]. In that
case the woman promised to leave her job, to refrain from marriage, to be a
companion to the man, and to make a permanent home for him; he agreed to
support the woman and her child for life. The Court of Appeal held the agreement
invalid as a contract in restraint of marriage (Civ. Code, § 1676) and, alternatively,
as "contrary to good morals" (Civ. Code, § 1607). The opinion does not state that
sexual relations formed any part of the consideration for the contract, nor explain
how—unless the contract called for sexual relations—the woman's employment
as a companion and housekeeper could be contrary to good morals.

The alternative holding in *Heaps* v. *Toy, supra,* finding the contract in that case
contrary to good morals, is inconsistent with the numerous California decisions
upholding contracts between nonmarital partners when such contracts are not
founded upon an illicit consideration, and is therefore disapproved.

consideration of sexual services not only represents the distilla-
tion of the decisional law, but also offers a far more precise and
workable standard than that advocated by defendant.) Our recent
decision in *In re Marriage of Dawley* (1976) 17 Cal.3d 342 [131
Cal.Rptr. 3, 551 P. 2d 323] offers a close analogy. Rejecting the
contention that an antenuptial agreement is invalid if the parties
contemplated a marriage of short duration, we pointed out in
Dawley that a standard based upon the subjective contemplation
of the parties is uncertain and unworkable; such a test, we stated,
"might invalidate virtually all antenuptial agreements on the
ground that the parties contemplated dissolution . . . but it provides no principled basis for determining which antenuptial agreements offend public policy and which do not." (17 Cal.3d 342,
352.)

Similarly, in the present case a standard which inquires
whether an agreement is "involved" in or "contemplates" a nonmarital relationship is vague and unworkable. Virtually all agreements between nonmarital partners can be said to be "involved"
in some sense in the fact of their mutual sexual relationship, or to
"contemplate" the existence of that relationship. Thus defendant's proposed standards, if taken literally, might invalidate all
agreements between nonmarital partners, a result no one favors.
Moreover, those standards offer no basis to distinguish between
valid and invalid agreements. By looking not to such uncertain
tests, but only to the consideration underlying the agreement, we
provide the parties and the courts with a practical guide to determine when an agreement between nonmarital partners should be
enforced.

(5) Defendant secondly relies upon the ground suggested by
the trial court: that the 1964 contract violated public policy because it impaired the community property rights of Betty Marvin,
defendant's lawful wife. Defendant points out that his earnings
while living apart from his wife before rendition of the interlocutory decree were community property under 1964 statutory law
(former Civ. Code, §§ 169, 169.2)[7] and that defendant's agree-

[7] Sections 169 and 169.2 were replaced in 1970 by Civil Code section 5118. In
1972 section 5118 was amended to provide that the earnings and accumulations of
both spouses "while living separate and apart from the other spouse, are the
separate property of the spouse."

ment with plaintiff purported to transfer to her a half interest in that community property. But whether or not defendant's contract with plaintiff exceeded his authority as manager of the community property (see former Civ. Code, § 172), defendant's argument fails for the reason that an improper transfer of community property is not void *ab initio,* but merely voidable at the instance of the aggrieved spouse. See *Ballinger* v. *Ballinger* (1937) 9 Cal.2d 330, 334 [70 P.2d 629; *Trimble* v. *Trimble* (1933) 219 Cal. 340, 344 [26 P.2d 477].)

In the present case Betty Marvin, the aggrieved spouse, had the opportunity to assert her community property rights in the divorce action. (See *Babbitt* v. *Babbitt* (1955) 44 Cal.2d 289, 293 [282 P. 2d 1].) The interlocutory and final decrees in that action fix and limit her interest. Enforcement of the contract between plaintiff and defendant against property awarded to defendant by the divorce decree will not impair any right of Betty's, and thus is not on that account violative of public policy.[8]

(6) Defendant's third contention is noteworthy for the lack of authority advanced in its support. He contends that enforcement of the oral agreement between plaintiff and himself is barred by Civil Code section 5134, which provides that "All contracts for marriage settlements must be in writing. . . ." A marriage settlement, however, is an agreement in contemplation of marriage in which each party agrees to release or modify the property rights which would otherwise arise from the marriage. (See *Corker* v. *Corker* (1891) 87 Cal. 643, 648 [25 P. 922].) The contract at issue here does not conceivably fall within that definition, and thus is beyond the compass of section 5134.[9]

---

[8] Defendant also contends that the contract is invalid as an agreement to promote or encourage divorce. (See 1 Witkin, Summary of Cal. Law (8th ed.) pp. 390-392 and cases there cited.) The contract between plaintiff and defendant did not, however, by its terms require defendant to divorce Betty, nor reward him for so doing. Moreover, the principle on which defendant relies does not apply when the marriage in question is beyond redemption (*Glickman* v. *Collins* (1975) 13 Cal.3d 852, 858-859 [120 Cal.Rptr. 76, 533 P.2d 204]); whether or not defendant's marriage to Betty was beyond redemption when defendant contracted with plaintiff is obviously a question of fact which cannot be resolved by judgment on the pleadings.

[9] Our review of the many cases enforcing agreements between nonmarital partners reveals that the majority of such agreements were oral. In two cases (*Fer-*

(7) Defendant finally argues that enforcement of the contract is barred by Civil Code section 43.5, subdivision (d), which provides that "No cause of action arises for . . . breach of promise of marriage." This rather strained contention proceeds from the premise that a promise of marriage impliedly includes a promise to support and to pool property acquired after marriage (see *Boyd* v. *Boyd* (1964) 228 Cal.App.2d 374 [39 Cal.Rptr. 400]) to the conclusion that pooling and support agreements not part of or accompanied by promise of marriage are barred by the section. We conclude that section 43.5 is not reasonably susceptible to the interpretation advanced by defendant, a conclusion demonstrated by the fact that since section 43.5 was enacted in 1939, numerous cases have enforced pooling agreements between nonmarital partners, and in none did court or counsel refer to section 43.5.

(3b) In summary, we base our opinion on the principle that adults who voluntarily live together and engage in sexual relations are nonetheless as competent as any other persons to contract respecting their earnings and property rights. Of course, they cannot lawfully contract to pay for the performance of sexual services, for such a contract is, in essence, an agreement for prostitution and unlawful for that reason. But they may agree to pool their earnings and to hold all property acquired during the relationship in accord with the law governing community property; conversely they may agree that each partner's earnings and the property acquired from those earnings remains the separate property of the earning partner.[10] So long as the agreement does not rest upon illicit meretricious consideration, the parties may order their economic affairs as they choose, and no policy precludes the courts from enforcing such agreements.

---

guson v. *Schuenemann, supra,* 167 Cal.App.2d 413; *Cline* v. *Festersen, supra,* 128 Cal.App.2d 380), the court expressly rejected defenses grounded upon the statute of frauds.

[10] A great variety of other arrangements are possible. The parties might keep their earnings and property separate, but agree to compensate one party for services which benefit the other. They may choose to pool only part of their earnings and property, to form a partnership or joint venture, or to hold property acquired as joint tenants or tenants in common, or agree to any other such arrangement. (See generally Weitzman, *Legal Regulation of Marriage: Tradition and Change* (1974) 62 Cal.L.Rev. 1169.)

In the present instance, plaintiff alleges that the parties agreed to pool their earnings, that they contracted to share equally in all property acquired, and that defendant agreed to support plaintiff. The terms of the contract as alleged do not rest upon any unlawful consideration.) We therefore conclude that the complaint furnishes a suitable basis upon which the trial court can render declaratory relief. (See 3 Witkin, Cal. Procedure (2d ed.) pp. 2335-2336.) The trial court consequently erred in granting defendant's motion for judgment on the pleadings.

3. (8a) *Plaintiff's complaint can be amended to state a cause of action founded upon theories of implied contract or equitable relief.*

As we have noted, both causes of action in plaintiff's complaint allege an express contract; neither asserts any basis for relief independent from the contract. In *In re Marriage of Cary, supra,* 34 Cal.App.3d 345, however, the Court of Appeal held that, in view of the policy of the Family Law Act, property accumulated by nonmarital partners in an actual family relationship should be divided equally. Upon examining the *Cary* opinion, the parties to the present case realized that plaintiff's alleged relationship with defendant might arguably support a cause of action independent of any express contract between the parties. The parties have therefore briefed and discussed the issue of the property rights of a nonmarital partner in the absence of an express contract. Although our conclusion that plaintiff's complaint states a cause of action based on an express contract alone compels us to reverse the judgment for defendant, resolution of the *Cary* issue will serve both to guide the parties upon retrial and to resolve a conflict presently manifest in published Court of Appeal decisions.

Both plaintiff and defendant stand in broad agreement that the law should be fashioned to carry out the reasonable expectations of the parties. Plaintiff, however, presents the following contentions: that the decisions prior to *Cary* rest upon implicit and erroneous notions of punishing a party for his or her guilt in entering into a nonmarital relationship, that such decisions result in an inequitable distribution of property accumulated during the relationship, and that *Cary* correctly held that the enactment of the Family Law Act in 1970 overturned those prior decisions. Defendant in response maintains that the prior decisions merely applied common law principles of contract and property to persons who have deliberately elected to remain outside the bounds of the community property system.[11] *Cary,* defendant contends, erred in holding that the Family Law Act vitiated the force of the prior precedents.

As we shall see from examination of the pre-*Cary* decisions, the truth lies somewhere between the positions of plaintiff and defendant. The classic opinion on this subject is *Vallera* v. *Vallera, supra,* 21 Cal.2d 681. Speaking for a four-member majority, Justice Traynor posed the question: "whether a woman living with a man as his wife but with no genuine belief that she is legally married to him acquires by reason of cohabitation alone the rights of a co-tenant in his earnings and accumulations during the period of their relationship." (21 Cal.2d at p. 684.) Citing *Flanagan* v. *Capital Nat. Bank* (1931) 213 Cal. 664 [3 P. 2d 307], which held that a nonmarital "wife" could not claim that her husband's estate was community property, the majority answered that question "in the negative." (Pp. 684-685.) *Vallera* explains that "Equitable considerations arising from the reasonable expectation of the continuation of benefits attending the status of marriage entered into in good faith are not present in such a case." (P. 685.) In the absence of express contract, *Vallera* concluded, the woman is entitled to share in property jointly accumulated *only* "in the proportion that her funds contributed toward its acquisition." (P. 685.) Justice Curtis, dissenting, ar-

---

[11] We note that a deliberate decision to avoid the strictures of the community property system is not the only reason that couples live together without marriage. Some couples may wish to avoid the permanent commitment that marriage implies, yet be willing to share equally any property acquired during the relationship; others may fear the loss of pension, welfare, or tax benefits resulting from marriage (see *Beckman* v. *Mayhew, supra,* 49 Cal.App.3d 529). Others may engage in the relationship as a possible prelude to marriage. In lower socio-economic groups the difficulty and expense of dissolving a former marriage often leads couples to choose a nonmarital relationship; many unmarried couples may also incorrectly believe that the doctrine of common law marriage prevails in California, and thus that they are in fact married. Consequently we conclude that the mere fact that a couple have not participated in a valid marriage ceremony cannot serve as a basis for a court's inference that the couple intend to keep their earnings and property separate and independent; the parties' intention can only be ascertained by a more searching inquiry into the nature of their relationship.

gued that the evidence showed an implied contract under which each party owned an equal interest in property acquired during the relationship.

The majority opinion in *Vallera* did not expressly bar recovery based upon an implied contract, nor preclude resort to equitable remedies. But *Vallera*'s broad assertion that equitable considerations "are not present" in the case of a nonmarital relationship (21 Cal.2d at p. 685) led the Courts of Appeal to interpret the language to preclude recovery based on such theories. (See *Lazzarevich* v. *Lazzarevich* (1948) 88 Cal.App.2d 708, 719 [200 P.2d 49]; *Oakley* v. *Oakley* (1947) 82 Cal.App.2d 188, 191-192 [185 P.2d 848].)[12]

Consequently, when the issue of the rights of a nonmarital partner reached this court in *Keene* v. *Keene* (1962) 57 Cal.2d 657 [21 Cal.Rptr. 593, 371 P.2d 329], the claimant forwent reliance upon theories of contract implied in law or fact. Asserting that she had worked on her partner's ranch and that her labor had enhanced its value, she confined her cause of action to the claim that the court should impress a resulting trust on the property derived from the sale of the ranch. The court limited its opinion accordingly, rejecting her argument on the ground that the rendition of services gives rise to a resulting trust only when the services aid in acquisition of the property, not in its subsequent improvement. (57 Cal.2d at p. 668.) Justice Peters, dissenting, attacked the majority's distinction between the rendition of services and the contribution of funds or property; he maintained that both property and services furnished valuable consideration, and potentially afforded the ground for a resulting trust.

This failure of the courts to recognize an action by a nonmarital partner based upon implied contract, or to grant an equitable remedy, contrasts with the judicial treatment of the putative spouse. Prior to the enactment of the Family Law Act, no statute

---

[12] The cases did not clearly determine whether a nonmarital partner could recover in quantum meruit for the reasonable value of services rendered. But when we affirmed a trial court ruling denying recovery in *Hill* v. *Estate of Westbrook, supra,* 39 Cal.2d 458, we did so in part on the ground that whether the partner "rendered her services because of expectation of monetary reward" (p. 462) was a question of fact resolved against her by the trial court—thus implying that in a proper case the court would allow recovery based on quantum meruit.

granted rights to a putative spouse.[13] The courts accordingly fashioned a variety of remedies by judicial decision. Some cases permitted the putative spouse to recover half the property on a theory that the conduct of the parties implied an agreement of partnership or joint venture. (See *Estate of Vargas* (1974) 36 Cal.App.3d 714, 717-718 [111 Cal.Rptr. 779]; *Sousa* v. *Freitas* (1970) 10 Cal.App.3d 660, 666 [89 Cal.Rptr. 485].) Others permitted the spouse to recover the reasonable value of rendered services, less the value of support received. (See *Sanguinetti* v. *Sanguinetti* (1937) 9 Cal.2d 95, 100-102 [69 P.2d 845, 111 A.L.R. 342].)[14] Finally, decisions affirmed the power of a court to employ equitable principles to achieve a fair division of property acquired during putative marriage. (*Coats* v. *Coats* (1911) 160 Cal. 671, 677-678 [118 P. 441]; *Caldwell* v. *Odisio* (1956) 142 Cal.App.2d 732, 735 [299 P.2d 14].)[15]

Thus in summary, the cases prior to *Cary* exhibited a schizophrenic inconsistency. By enforcing an express contract between nonmarital partners unless it rested upon an unlawful consideration, the courts applied a common law principle as to contracts. Yet the courts disregarded the common law principle that holds that implied contracts can arise from the conduct of the parties.[16] Refusing to enforce such contracts, the courts spoke of leaving

[13] The Family Law Act, in Civil Code section 4452, classifies property acquired during a putative marriage as " 'quasi-marital property,' " and requires that such property be divided upon dissolution of the marriage in accord with Civil Code section 4800.

[14] The putative spouse need not prove that he rendered services in expectation of monetary reward in order to recover the reasonable value of those services. (*Sanguinetti* v. *Sanguinetti, supra,* 9 Cal.2d 95, 100.)

[15] The contrast between principles governing nonmarital and putative relationships appears most strikingly in *Lazzarevich* v. *Lazzarevich, supra,* 88 Cal. App.2d 708. When Mrs. Lazzarevich sued her husband for divorce in 1945, she discovered to her surprise that she was not lawfully married to him. She nevertheless reconciled with him, and the Lazzareviches lived together for another year before they finally separated. The court awarded her recovery for the reasonable value of services rendered, less the value of support received, until she discovered the invalidity of the marriage, but denied recovery for the same services rendered after that date.

[16] Contracts may be express or implied. These terms however do not denote different kinds of contracts, but have reference to the evidence by which the agreement between the parties is shown. If the agreement is shown by the direct words of the parties, spoken or written, the contract is said to be an express one. But if such agreement can only be shown by the acts and conduct of the parties, interpreted in the light of the subject matter and of the surrounding circumstances,

the parties "in the position in which they had placed themselves" (*Oakley* v. *Oakley, supra,* 82 Cal.App.2d 188, 192), just as if they were guilty parties *in pari delicto.*

Justice Curtis noted this inconsistency in his dissenting opinion in *Vallera,* pointing out that "if an express agreement will be enforced, there is no legal or just reason why an implied agreement to share the property cannot be enforced." (21 Cal.2d 681, 686; see Bruch, *Property Rights of De Facto Spouses Including Thoughts of the Value of Homemakers' Services* (1976) 10 Family L.Q. 101, 117-121.) And in *Keene* v. *Keene, supra,* 57 Cal.2d 657, Justice Peters observed that if the man and woman "were not illegally living together . . . it would be a plain business relationship and a contract would be implied." (Dis. opn. at p. 672.)

Still another inconsistency in the prior cases arises from their treatment of property accumulated through joint effort. To the extent that a partner had contributed *funds* or *property,* the cases held that the partner obtains a proportionate share in the acquisition, despite the lack of legal standing of the relationship. (*Vallera* v. *Vallera, supra,* 21 Cal.2d at p. 685; see *Weak* v. *Weak, supra,* 202 Cal. App.2d 632,639.) Yet courts have refused to recognize just such an interest based upon the contribution of *services.* As Justice Curtis points out "Unless it can be argued that a woman's services as cook, housekeeper, and homemaker are valueless, it would seem logical that if, when she contributes money to the purchase of property, her interest will be protected, then when she contributes her services in the home, her interest in property accumulated should be protected." (*Vallera* v. *Vallera, supra,* 21 Cal.2d 681, 686-687 (*dis. opn.*); see Bruch, *op. cit., supra,* 10 Family L.Q. 101, 110-114; Article, *Illicit Cohabitation: The Impact of the Vallera and Keene Cases on the Rights of the Meretricious Spouse* (1973) 6 U.C. Davis L.Rev. 354, 369-370; Comment (1972) 48 Wash.L.Rev. 635,641.)

Thus as of 1973, the time of the filing of *In re Marriage of*

---

then the contract is an implied one." (*Skelly* v. *Bristol Sav. Bank* (1893) 63 Conn. 83 [26 A. 474], quoted in 1 Corbin, Contracts (1963) p. 41.) Thus, as Justice Schauer observed in *Desny* v. *Wilder* (1956) 46 Cal.2d 715 [299 P.2d 257], in a sense all contracts made in fact, as distinguished from quasi-contractual obligations, are express contracts, differing only in the manner in which the assent of the parties is expressed and proved. (See 46 Cal.2d at pp. 735-736.)

Cary, supra, 34 Cal.App.3d 345, the cases apparently held that a nonmarital partner who rendered services in the absence of express contract could assert no right to property acquired during that relationship. The facts of *Cary* demonstrated the unfairness of that rule.

Janet and Paul Cary had lived together, unmarried, for more than eight years. They held themselves out to friends and family as husband and wife, reared four children, purchased a home and other property, obtained credit, filed joint income tax returns, and otherwise conducted themselves as though they were married. Paul worked outside the home, and Janet generally cared for the house and children.

In 1971 Paul petitioned for "nullity of the marriage."[17] Following a hearing on that petition, the trial court awarded Janet half the property acquired during the relationship, although all such property was traceable to Paul's earnings. The Court of Appeal affirmed the award.

Reviewing the prior decisions which had denied relief to the homemaking partner, the Court of Appeal reasoned that those decisions rested upon a policy of punishing persons guilty of cohabitation without marriage. The Family Law Act, the court observed, aimed to eliminate fault or guilt as a basis for dividing marital property. But once fault or guilt is excluded, the court reasoned, nothing distinguishes the property rights of a nonmarital "spouse" from those of a putative spouse. Since the latter is entitled to half the " 'quasi marital property' " (Civ. Code, § 4452), the Court of Appeal concluded that, giving effect to the policy of the Family Law Act, a nonmarital cohabitator should also be entitled to half the property accumulated during an "actual family relationship." (34 Cal.App.3d at p. 353.)[18]

[17] The Court of Appeal opinion in *In re Marriage of Cary, supra,* does not explain why Paul Cary filed his action as a petition for nullity. Briefs filed with this court, however, suggest that Paul may have been seeking to assert rights as a putative spouse. In the present case, on the other hand, neither party claims the status of an actual or putative spouse. Under such circumstances an action to adjudge "the marriage" in the instant case a nullity would be pointless and could not serve as a device to adjudicate contract and property rights arising from the parties' nonmarital relationship. Accordingly, plaintiff here correctly chose to assert her rights by means of an ordinary civil action.

[18] The court in *Cary* also based its decision upon an analysis of Civil Code section 4452, which specifies the property rights of a putative spouse. Section

Cary met with a mixed reception in other appellate districts. In *Estate of Atherley, supra,* 44 Cal.App.3d 758, the Fourth District agreed with *Cary* that under the Family Law Act a nonmarital partner in an actual family relationship enjoys the same right to an equal division of property as a putative spouse. In *Beckman v. Mayhew, supra,* 49 Cal.App.3d 529, however, the Third District rejected *Cary* on the ground that the Family Law Act was

---

4452 states that if the "court finds that either party or both parties believed in good faith that the marriage was valid, the court should declare such party or parties to have the status of a putative spouse, and, . . . shall divide, in accordance with Section 4800, that property acquired during the union. . . ." Since section 4800 requires an equal division of community property, *Cary* interpreted section 4452 to require an equal division of the property of a putative marriage, so long as one spouse believed in good faith that the marriage was valid. Thus under section 4452, *Cary* concluded, the "guilty spouse" (the spouse who knows the marriage is invalid) has the same right to half the property as does the "innocent" spouse.

Cary then reasoned that if the "guilty" spouse to a putative marriage is entitled to one-half the marital property, the "guilty" partner in a nonmarital relationship should also receive one-half of the property. Otherwise, the court stated, "We should be obliged to presume a legislative intent that a person, who by deceit leads another to believe a valid marriage exists between them, shall be legally guaranteed half of the property they acquire even though most, or all, may have resulted from the earnings of the blameless partner. At the same time we must infer an inconsistent legislative intent that two persons who, candidly with each other, enter upon an unmarried family relationship, shall be denied any judicial aid whatever in the assertion of otherwise valid property rights." (34 Cal.App.3d at p. 352.)

This reasoning in *Cary* has been criticized by commentators. (See Note, *op. cit., supra,* 25 Hastings L.J. 1226, 1234-1235; Comment, *In re Marriage of Cary* [*sic*]: *The End of the Putative-Meretricious Spouse Distinction in California* (1975) 12 San Diego L.Rev. 436, 444-446.) The commentators note that Civil Code section 4455 provides that an "innocent" party to a putative marriage can recover spousal support, from which they infer that the Legislature intended to give only the "innocent" spouse a right to one-half of the quasi-marital property under section 4452.

We need not now resolve this dispute concerning the interpretation of section 4452. Even if *Cary* is correct in holding that a "guilty" putative spouse has a right to one-half of the marital property, it does not necessarily follow that a nonmarital partner has an identical right. In a putative marriage the parties will arrange their economic affairs with the expectation that on dissolution the property will be divided equally. If a "guilty" putative spouse receives one-half of the property under section 4452, no expectation of the "innocent" spouse has been frustrated. In a nonmarital relationship, on the other hand, the parties may expressly or tacitly determine to order their economic relationship in some other manner, and to impose community property principles regardless of such understanding may frustrate the parties' expectations.

not intended to change California law dealing with nonmarital relationships.

(9) If *Cary* is interpreted as holding that the Family Law Act requires an equal division of property accumulated in nonmarital "actual family relationships," then we agree with *Beckman* v. *Mayhew* that *Cary* distends the act. No language in the Family Law Act addresses the property rights of nonmarital partners, and nothing in the legislative history of the act suggests that the Legislature considered that subject.[19] The delineation of the rights of nonmarital partners before 1970 had been fixed entirely by judicial decision; we see no reason to believe that the Legislature, by enacting the Family Law Act, intended to change that state of affairs.

But although we reject the reasoning of *Cary* and *Atherley*, we share the perception of the *Cary* and *Atherley* courts that the application of former precedent in the factual setting of those cases would work an unfair distribution of the property accumulated by the couple. Justice Friedman in *Beckman* v. *Mayhew*, *supra*, 49 Cal.App.3d 529, 535, also questioned the continued viability of our decisions in *Vallera* and *Keene*; commentators have argued the need to reconsider those precedents.[20] We should not, therefore, reject the authority of *Cary* and *Atherley* without also examining the deficiencies in the former law which led to those decisions.

The principal reason why the pre-*Cary* decisions result in an unfair distribution of property inheres in the court's refusal to permit a nonmarital partner to assert rights based upon accepted principles of implied contract or equity. We have examined the reasons advanced to justify this denial of relief, and find that none have merit.

First, we note that the cases denying relief to not rest their

---

[19] Despite the extensive material available on the legislative history of the Family Law Act neither *Cary* nor plaintiff cites any reference which suggests that the Legislature ever considered the issue of the property rights of nonmarital partners, and our independent examination has uncovered no such reference.

[20] See Bruch, *op. cit., supra,* 10 Family L.Q. 101, 113; Article, *op. cit., supra,* 6 U.C. Davis L.Rev. 354; Comment (1975) 6 Golden Gate L.Rev. 179, 197-201; Comment, *op. cit., supra,* 12 San Diego L.Rev. 436; Note, *op. cit., supra,* 25 Hastings L.J. 1226, 1246.

refusal upon any theory of "punishing" a "guilty" partner. Indeed, to the extent that denial of relief "punishes" one partner, it necessarily rewards the other by permitting him to retain a disproportionate amount of the property. Concepts of "guilt" thus cannot justify an unequal division of property between two equally "guilty" persons.[21]

Other reasons advanced in the decisions fare no better. The principal argument seems to be that "[e]quitable considerations arising from the reasonable expectation of . . . benefits attending the status of marriage . . . are not present [in a nonmarital relationship]." (*Vallera* v. *Vallera, supra,* 21 Cal.2d at p. 685.) But, although parties to a nonmarital relationship obviously cannot have based any expectations upon the belief that they were married, other expectations and equitable considerations remain. The parties may well expect that property will be divided in accord with the parties' own tacit understanding and that in the absence of such understanding the courts will fairly apportion property accumulated through mutual effort. We need not treat nonmarital partners as putatively married persons in order to apply principles of implied contract, or extend equitable remedies; we need to treat them only as we do any other unmarried persons.[22]

---

[21] Justice Finley of the Washington Supreme Court explains: "Under such circumstances [the dissolution of a nonmarital relationship], this court and the courts of other jurisdictions have, in effect, sometimes said, 'We will wash our hands of such disputes. The parties should and must be left to their own devices, just where they find themselves.' To me, such pronouncements seem overly fastidious and a bit fatuous. They are unrealistic and, among other things, ignore the fact that an unannounced (but nevertheless effective and binding) rule of law is inherent in any such terminal statements by a court of law. The unannounced but inherent rule is simply that the party who has title, or in some instances who is in possession, will enjoy the rights of ownership of the property concerned. The rule often operates to the great advantage of the cunning and the shrewd, who wind up with possession of the property, or title to it in their names, at the end of a so-called meretricious relationship. So, although the courts proclaim that they will have nothing to do with such matters, the proclamation in itself establishes, as to the parties involved, an effective and binding rule of law which tends to operate purely by accident or perhaps by reason of the cunning, anticipatory designs of just one of the parties." (*West* v. *Knowles* (1957) 50 Wn.2d 311 [311 P.2d 689, 692] (conc. opn.).)

[22] In some instances a confidential relationship may arise between nonmarital partners, and economic transactions between them should be governed by the principles applicable to such relationships.

The remaining arguments advanced from time to time to deny remedies to the nonmarital partners are of less moment. There is no more reason to presume that services are contributed as a gift than to presume that funds are contributed as a gift; in any event the better approach is to presume, as Justice Peters suggested, "that the parties intend to deal fairly with each other." (*Keene* v. *Keene, supra,* 57 Cal.2d 657, 674 (dissenting opn.); see Bruch, *op. cit., supra,* 10 Family L.Q. 101, 113.)

The argument that granting remedies to the nonmarital partners would discourage marriage must fail; as *Cary* pointed out, "with equal or greater force the point might be made that the pre-1970 rule was calculated to cause the income-producing partner to avoid marriage and thus retain the benefit of all of his or her accumulated earnings." (34 Cal.App.3d at p. 353.) Although we recognize the well-established public policy to foster and promote the institution of marriage (see *Deyoe* v. *Superior Court* (1903) 140 Cal. 476, 482 [74 P. 28]), perpetuation of judicial rules which result in an inequitable distribution of property accumulated during a nonmarital relationship is neither a just nor an effective way of carrying out that policy.

We are aware that many young couples live together without the solemnization of marriage, in order to make sure that they can successfully later undertake marriage. This trial period,[23] preliminary to marriage, serves as some assurance that the marriage will not subsequently end in dissolution to the harm of both parties. We are aware, as we have stated, of the pervasiveness of nonmarital relationships in other situations.

The mores of the society have indeed changed so radically in regard to cohabitation that we cannot impose a standard based on alleged moral considerations that have apparently been so widely abandoned by so many. Lest we be misunderstood, however, we take this occasion to point out that the structure of society itself largely depends upon the institution of marriage, and nothing we have said in this opinion should be taken to derogate from that institution. The joining of the man and woman in marriage is at once the most socially productive and individually fulfilling relationship that one can enjoy in the course of a lifetime.

---

[23] Toffler, Future Shock (Bantam Books, 1971) page 253.

(8b) We conclude that the judicial barriers that may stand in the way of a policy based upon the fulfillment of the reasonable expectations of the parties to a nonmarital relationship should be removed. As we have explained, the courts now hold that express agreements will be enforced unless they rest on an unlawful meretricious consideration. We add that in the absence of an express agreement, the courts may look to a variety of other remedies in order to protect the parties' lawful expectations.[24]

The courts may inquire into the conduct of the parties to determine whether that conduct demonstrates an implied contract or implied agreement of partnership or joint venture (see *Estate of Thornton* (1972) 81 Wn.2d 72 [499 P.2d 864]), or some other tacit understanding between the parties. The courts may, when appropriate, employ principles of constructive trust (see *Omer* v. *Omer* (1974) 11 Wash.App. 386 [523 P.2d 957] or resulting trust (see *Hyman* v. *Hyman* (Tex.Civ.App. 1954) 275 S.W.2d 149). Finally, a nonmarital partner may recover in quantum meruit for the reasonable value of household services rendered less the reasonable value of support received if he can show that he rendered services with the expectation of monetary reward. (See *Hill* v. *Estate of Westbrook, supra,* 39 Cal.2d 458, 462.)[25]

Since we have determined that plaintiff's complaint states a cause of action for breach of an express contract, and, as we have explained, can be amended to state a cause of action independent of allegations of express contract,[26] we must conclude that the trial court erred in granting defendant a judgment on the pleadings.

---

[24] We do not seek to resurrect the doctrine of common law marriage, which was abolished in California by statute in 1895. (See *Norman* v. *Thompson* (1898) 121 Cal. 620, 628 [54 P. 143]; *Estate of Abate* (1958) 166 Cal.App.2d 282, 292 [333 P.2d 200].) Thus we do not hold that plaintiff and defendant were "married," nor do we extend to plaintiff the rights which the Family Law Act grants valid or putative spouses; we hold only that she has the same rights to enforce contracts and to assert her equitable interest in property acquired through her effort as does any other unmarried person.

[25] Our opinion does not preclude the evolution of additional equitable remedies to protect the expectations of the parties to a nonmarital relationship in cases in which existing remedies prove inadequate; the suitability of such remedies may be determined in later cases in light of the factual setting in which they arise.

[26] We do not pass upon the question whether, in the absence of an express or implied contractual obligation, a party to a nonmarital relationship is entitled to support payments from the other party after the relationship terminates.

The judgment is reversed and the cause remanded for further proceedings consistent with the views expressed herein.[27]

Wright, C.J., McComb, J., Mosk, J., Sullivan, J., and Richardson, J., concurred.

CLARK, J., Concurring and Dissenting—The majority opinion properly permit recovery on the basis of either express or implied in fact agreement between the parties. These being the issues presented, their resolution requires reversal of the judgment. Here, the opinion should stop.

This court should not attempt to determine all anticipated rights, duties and remedies within every meretricious relationship —particularly in vague terms. Rather, these complex issues should be determined as each arises in a concrete case.

The majority broadly indicate that a party to a meretricious relationship may recover on the basis of equitable principles and in quantum meruit. However, the majority fail to advise us of the circumstances permitting recovery, limitations on recovery, or whether their numerous remedies are cumulative or exclusive. Conceivably, under the majority opinion a party may recover half of the property acquired during the relationship on the basis of general equitable principles, recover a bonus based on specific equitable considerations, and recover a second bonus in quantum meruit.

The general sweep of the majority opinion raises but fails to answer several questions. First, because the Legislature specifically excluded some parties to a meretricious relationship from the equal division rule of Civil Code section 4452, is this court now free to create an equal division rule? Second, upon termination of the relationship, is it equitable to impose the economic obligations of lawful spouses on meretricious parties when the latter may have rejected matrimony to avoid such obligations? Third, does not application of equitable principles—necessitating examination of the conduct of the parties—violate the spirit of the Family Law Act of 1969, designed to eliminate the bitterness and acrimony resulting from the former fault system in divorce? Fourth, will not application of equitable principles reimpose upon

[27] We wish to commend the parties and amici for the exceptional quality of the briefs and argument in this case.

trial courts the unmanageable burden of arbitrating domestic disputes? Fifth, will not a quantum meruit system of compensation for services—discounted by benefits received—place meretricious spouses in a better position than lawful spouses? Sixth, if a quantum meruit system is to be allowed, does fairness not require inclusion of all services and all benefits regardless of how difficult the evaluation?

When the parties to a meretricious relationship show by express or implied in fact agreement they intend to create mutual obligations, the courts should enforce the agreement. However, in the absence of agreement, we should stop and consider the ramifications before creating economic obligations which may violate legislative intent, contravene the intention of the parties, and surely generate undue burdens on our trial courts.

By judicial overreach, the majority perform a nunc pro tunc marriage, dissolve it, and distribute its property on terms never contemplated by the parties, case law or the Legislature.

INDEX

INDEX

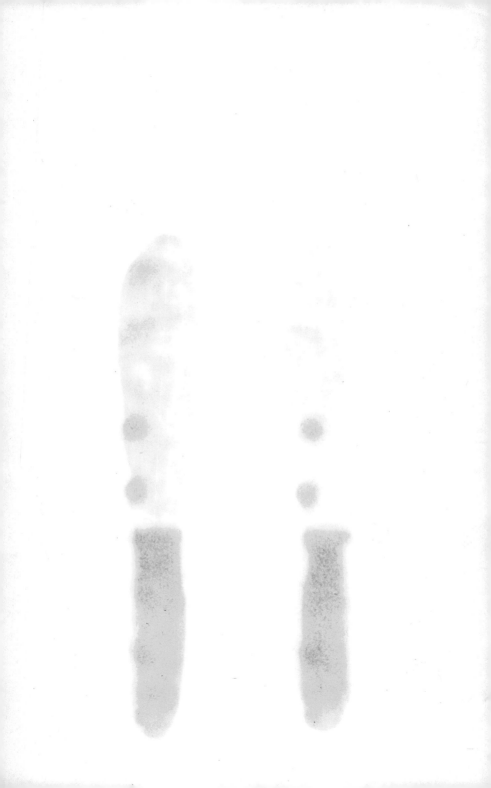